Ordering Information

The paperback sourcebooks listed below are published quarterly and can be ordered either by subscription or single-copy.

Subscriptions cost $40.00 per year for institutions, agencies, and libraries. Individuals can subscribe at the special rate of $30.00 per year *if payment is by personal check.* (Note that the full rate of $40.00 applies if payment is by institutional check, even if the subscription is designated for an individual.) Standing orders are accepted.

Single copies are available at $9.95 when payment accompanies order, and *all single-copy orders under $25.00 must include payment.* (California, New Jersey, New York, and Washington, D.C., residents please include appropriate sales tax.) For billed orders, cost per copy is $9.95 plus postage and handling. (Prices subject to change without notice.)

Bulk orders (ten or more copies) of any individual sourcebook are available at the following discounted prices: 10–49 copies, $8.95 each; 50–100 copies, $7.96 each; over 100 copies, *inquire.* Sales tax and postage and handling charges apply as for single copy orders.

To ensure correct and prompt delivery, all orders must give either the *name of an individual* or an *official purchase order number.* Please submit your order as follows:

Subscriptions: specify series and year subscription is to begin.
Single Copies: specify sourcebook code (such as, CD1) and first two words of title.

Mail orders for United States and Possessions, Latin America, Canada, Japan, Australia, and New Zealand to:
Jossey-Bass Inc., Publishers
433 California Street
San Francisco, California 94104

Mail orders for all other parts of the world to:
Jossey-Bass Limited
28 Banner Street
London EC1Y 8QE

New Directions for Child Development Series
William Damon, *Editor-in-Chief*

Contents

Editor's Notes

Early experience is an ancient and persistant problem in the study of human development. Plato (Hamilton and Cairns, 1980) made the early years a cornerstone of his grand plan for educating the populace in his ideal society. Comenius, the great seventeenth-century educator, developed an entire curriculum for infants to begin at their mother's knee. And one of the great forerunners of scientific psychology, John Locke, saw development beginning at birth with a blank slate, a tabula rasa, on which experiences were inscribed to shape development (Fowler, 1983; Raymont, 1937). In the heyday of early behaviorism in the 1920s, John Watson (1957) made claims for determining the personal destiny of adult competence by analyzing the manner in which the child had been educated from birth, regardless of background.

Until comparatively recently, most formulations were simply grand claims supported by strong beliefs in the importance of environment and in the common sense notions that what happens in the first years will exercise a significant influence on subsequent development. While playing an important role in freeing human thought from the shackles of entrenched religious and philosophical views of human development as preformed or predetermined by God, the fates, or biology (Hunt, 1961), systematic studies on the role of experience, let alone early experience, did not begin until this century. And, though Montessori (1967) defined early development as a sensitive period for learning in children as early as the turn of the century, research interest in the problem of early critical or sensitive periods began first with studies on lower animals (Scott, 1978). Interest in early learning and early experience spread during the 1920s and 1930s to studies of young children, but most of the work was empirically driven, with little formal theorizing.

Research was undertaken in several frameworks, each limiting the results and the nature of understanding that could be expected (Fowler, 1962a, 1983). Perhaps the largest body of research came out of a kind of 'social action research intended to demonstrate the value of nursery school education to the mental development of young children. The results generally showed small and inconsequential IQ gains for nursery school children compared with home staying controls. Outcomes were inevitably limited by the fact that the programs were poorly defined and centered on perceptual motor and social play, while development was assessed by IQ tests that yielded a single index, heavily weighted in abstract verbal and logical skills. Most of the children who attended nursery schools, moreover, came from advantaged, well-educated families whose home life was

1

already rich in concepts of both the school programs and the IQ tests. Only among children from less educated homes or where development was assessed on mental tests weighted toward perceptual motor and spatial skills were more substantial gains realized.

A second type of research was inspired by the behaviorist outlook of the period. Much of this research was conducted with white rats in the laboratory, and those studies undertaken with children were aimed more at proving general laws of learning than at addressing developmental questions. Many studies were designed to determine the ages at which children could learn various concepts, including the conditionability of infants, and studies were inherently limited by a theoretical mistrust of internal mental processes that impeded conceptions of the child as an active, organized system that changed with experience over time. Concern for scientific rigor mechanically aping the natural sciences, coupled with a reductionist, molecular framework, tended to generate variable-oriented studies on learning arbitrary small bits of information abstracted from a particular context (motor responses such as lever pulling or digit memory tasks). Short-term learning of isolated variables did not lead to much information on how experience influences development, let alone on how early experience might influence the development of competence.

A third major body of research, which was pursued and inspired by the formulations of the Gesell "laboratories," was framed in terms of the relative importance of maturation and learning for development. Although a number of studies on young children involved issues of early training, the framework was more broadly conceived in terms of nature versus nurture, an issue that has long preoccupied psychology, as it does today, if in the modern dress of biogenetic expression and psychobiology (Haith and Campos, 1983). Gesell was a passionate advocate of the predominance of maturation in development, believing experience merely served to deflect the internal workings of the biological unfolding in small ways. The results of the collected experimental training studies conducted by Gesell and his students, a number of them by the method of co-twin control on a single pair of identical twins during infancy and early childhood, were interpreted as supporting the importance of maturation over learning. As analyzed elsewhere (Fowler, 1962a, 1983), however, the short-term nature of the studies, the relatively simple tasks inherently limited by ceiling effects, and the tendency to overlook how general experience of the control twin (or group), and not maturation alone, was contributing to development, negated many of Gesell's conclusions. Moreover, careful scrutiny of the data indicated that in fact the trained twin or group often gained decided advantages from the earlier training, some of which lasted into later development (Fowler, 1962a, 1983; Razel, 1985), and that in any case experience was in fact a major source of development in both experimental and control group children.

Nevertheless, occasional studies, more concerned with exploring the potentials of early training, have generally demonstrated the impact that more significant forms of experience may have on development. Among these were training studies of musical skills (Jersild and Bienstock, 1931, 1934), of motor skills (McGraw, 1935, 1939), of language (Dawe, 1942; Fowler, 1983), and of early reading (Davidson, 1931; Fowler, 1962b; 1983). Focusing on an integrated set of concepts in a domain of knowledge or skill, rather than on either trivial skills or global knowledge (IQ), these studies have furnished important heuristic evidence on the role of early experience in the development of competence.

Aside from these scattered studies, a large portion of research on children's development at any age, again initially inspired by Gesell, has been and continues to be devoted to collecting information on children's characteristics at various points in development, as opposed to tracing the influences of experience on development. Research since the discoveries of Piaget, however, following World War II, has become more sophisticated in asking questions about the cognitive mechanisms involved in children's functioning, rather than simply listing or describing age-linked characteristics as the earlier Gesell-inspired researchers had.

It was not until after World War II, with the confluence of several strands of research—including a growing body of studies on perceptual and social deprivation (Casler, 1961; Yarrow, 1961), as well as work on early education, early training, maturation versus learning, and psychoanalytic theory (Orlansky, 1949)—with emerging political currents (for example, the Civil Rights Movement), that more studies began to be formulated in terms of early development as a special period for experience to influence development. Perhaps the biggest boost to this theoretical outlook came from the seminal book of Hebb (1949), *The Organization of Behavior,* in which he synthesized existing research and presented a conceptual model on the long-term impact early experience has on mental development. Much of the evidence for his thesis was derived from a growing body of research on the long-term deleterious effects of early sensory deprivation, much of it conducted on lower animals. But Hebb also drew on the work on sensory defects and brain damage in humans, which showed similar patterns. Hunt's (1961) classic, *Intelligence and Experience,* and Fowler's (1962a) extensive review of *Cognitive Learning in Infancy and Early Childhood,* served to galvanize and extend interest in the problem.

The waves of research that followed these formulations, however, unlike the research of the prewar period, included a smaller proportion of studies addressed to the basic problem. The bulk of research energy was poured into a national effort of social action research, early educational intervention in the form of Head-Start-type programs designed to solve the widespread social problem of children from ghettoes and poor communities who failed in school more frequently than children from socioeconomically advantaged classes did (Zigler and Valentine, 1979). Numerous formal research programs were undertaken in this context, along with a myriad of community programs, but considerations of experimental control and focus on theoretically defined issues bearing on the role of early experience in the development of competence were secondary to the social goals of improving the lot of the poor (Fowler, 1983). Thus, in the interest of cost-benefit considerations (though not originally or formally defined in this way), most of the educational programs began at ages three and four, in the belief that this was early enough to make a substantial difference, though from the theoretical point of view of the issue of early experience, this was *after* the child's cognitive foundation had already been fairly well established. Few studies began earlier, almost none during early infancy, and among all studies, comparisons of age of starting educational programs were generally confounded with duration of experience (Fowler, 1983; Palmer and Andersen, 1979).

The most important constraint, however, remained the imposition of a formal curriculum on special populations with little regard to their cultural characteristics and community circumstances. Young children were removed from the context of their community for a comparatively short segment of their lives (a few months or a year or two), then returned to adapt to the very different and difficult circumstances of their way of life and their poverty as best they could. Second, like the earlier research on the nursery school, much of the research engaged broad-based, global curricula and utilized the IQ test as a criterion of cognitive development, which effectively masked relations between the specifics of experience and the particulars of competence realized. The general results of this vast accumulation of social action research are of course well known. It is in many ways surprising that, given the plethora of problems, positive influences on the development of competence, in the form of modest superiority over controls in reading and mathematics achievement and in indices of school motivation and participation, could be evident even as far as late adolescence, years after the early intervention programs had terminated (Consortium for Longitudinal Studies, 1983).

Curiously, despite the accrual of large bodies of studies on various early life influences in various developmental periods, there are remarkably few studies of human development addressed specifically to this question, as my recent survey has shown (Fowler, 1983). Aside from the early intervention research, much of the research has continued to center on characterizing rather than on tracing the sources of development at various ages, albeit more analytically than the descriptive norm gathering of the Gesell era. Large bodies of studies have followed either of two formats—research on familial and other social factors influencing development, not explicitly addressed to age, or studies devoted to demonstrating or questioning various aspects of the validity of the Piagetian theory of cognitive development. (There is of course the large body of research, growing in the past decade, on biogenetic influences on development, obviously a quite different concern.)

The first type of format is inherently limited by the difficulty of linking ages with the patterns of influence studied in the mainly cross-sectional correlation and regression strategies utilized. Although research in recent years has become increasing sophisticated in the use of path analyses that tie the phenomena observed to age periods, this is not quite the same as tracing the effect of patterns of influence in children over the course of developmental cycles, which requires more costly and time-consuming longitudinal investments. Research in the second format, followed by investigators who have in one way or another challenged Piagetian theory on the timing and sequence of cognitive developmental acquisitions, has been centered on whether the child may have certain cognitive skills, such as number (Gelman and Gallistel, 1978), object permanence (Siegel and Brainerd, 1978), and conservation (Brainerd, 1977; Bryant, 1974), earlier than Piagetian formulations hold. Although often concerned with demonstrating the cognitive learning capabilities as well as the congitive competences of infants and young children, and thus bearing on the question of early experience, this strategy is not really addressed to the question of how and how much early experience influences development and the development of competence, especially with reference to its impact over long time spans.

The biggest problem in studying the effects of early experience is to identify phenomena of a magnitude sufficient to make a long-term impact on development in the context of a continuing accumulation of multiple, competing experiences. Just what are the boundaries of early experience? The problem is certainly not defined merely by what learning can occur during infancy and early childhood. The facts of early learning are easy to document, but they only take on siginificance as they appear to occupy a permanent place in the scheme of the developmental cycle. Even if we assume that the first five years of life fall within the definition of early experience, five years constitute only about 25 percent of the span of the formative years, from birth to adulthood (about age twenty), and only about 7 percent of the traditional seventy-year life span, which as we now know (Baltes and Reese, 1984) involves learning and change to the very end.

One obvious strategy for tackling the difficulty of identifying which early experiences have such lasting effects is to study the effects of early experiences that vary markedly from the experiential norms or modes for a population in question. Such experiences can of course contrast sharply in either of two directions. They can be either lesser or greater in strength (or even be completely absent or present) than the experiences defining the usual course of early life. Research on the long-term effects of perceptual and other forms of early deprivation illustrates the first direction, including studies on the effects of maternal or institutional deprivation (Casler, 1961; Yarrow, 1961). Research on children from highly advantaged families with cognitively enriched environments illustrates the second direction. The body of early intervention research, in furnishing enrichment experiences in the early years to poor children that contrasts sharply with the experiential norms of their impoverished environments, furnishes another illustration following the second direction.

For a variety of reasons, largely concerning social policy, the bulk of research on early experience has concentrated on children from less advantaged environments. In this sense, most of the research has studied children whose main bodies of experience are widely considered cognitively less advantaged or at least quite different than those of the mainstream middle-class populations from socioeconomically well-off homes. The studies of the effects of nursery school experiences on middle-class children in the 1920s and 1930s are an exception, though a handful of investigators have devoted special attention to the phenomena of intellectual precocity, largely concentrated on children from decidedly well-educated homes (Bloom, 1985; Feldman, 1980; Fowler, 1983; Gardner, 1983).

The experiences of early life can be manipulated in ways other than those of presence-absence or intensity—especially those of timing and duration—but also in terms of any of a myriad of the forms of interaction and cognitive transactions with the social and physical environment. As is evident from the social policy constraints and the limited body of work directly on early experience, except with lower animals (Denenberg and Bell, 1960), few studies on early learning making use of these various refinements have been undertaken (Fowler, 1983). One of the few studies of this kind was explicitly designed to test the effects of varying the age at which intensive early stimulation is introduced. Swenson (see Fowler, 1983, Vol. 2) found that infants who were stimulated intensively in regard to language beginning at three months gained a significant advantage in language devlopment over infants whose intensive stiumlation began at eight months. The advantage was maintained, however, only in those infants whose parents continued the intensive involvement in language interaction with their infants after the formal twelve-month program terminated.

The chapters assembled in this issue have taken various approaches to the problem of how early experience influences the development of competence, but they also group themselves into three main themes that also weave together in certain ways. The first three chapters, by authors Caldwell, Hunt, and Sigel, are primarily concerned with how varying the conditions of early child care in institutional and home settings changes the level and type of competence the child develops. The next two chapters, one by Feldman and Goldsmith, the other by Fowler, in contrast, explore the question of how very special conditions of intellectual stimulation in the child's early home life may interact with biology and culture to generate exceptional levels of talent development. Finally, the last author, Peak, explores the question of the special role an entire culture may play in setting goals, expectations, and socialization modes beginning in the earliest periods of development to accelerate the development of social competence and learning skills. At one time cultural influence was widely studied in the realm of child care and national character or culture and personality with uncertain resolution. Peak suggests an interacting role between culture and development in which later and early experiences complement one another in a total cultural framework of institutional values and patterns.

With respect to their special concerns, Caldwell has focused on the issue of group day care for infants and young children as an environment offering an important type of early experiences that, depending on quality, will differentially influence the young child's development. She reviews briefly the research on day care, which generally indicates that young children can fare well cognitively, socioemotionally, and in health and physical development at least for the short-term. She argues cogently that the social realities of today's world require putting in place a system of professionally run group care for young children, whose quality would be maintained and improved through monitoring and through research on short- and long-term effects on development.

Hunt compares the development of infants in orphanages with that of infants reared at home in different social-class settings. The special merit of the work resides in showing how altering specific conditions of child care will bring about important changes in cognitive developmental outcomes in different ways and across several cultures, with particular effects on the development of language. Among important conditions altered in various ways were the systematic improvement of child-care ratios, use of audiovisual stimulation devices, and special caregiver training focused especially on language.

Sigel's work consistently evaluates the positive effects of caregivers developing abstract, interactive inquiry modes of mental processing (distancing strategies) to facilitate the development of children's representational competence, both in the home and institutional settings and in different social classes and ethnic groups. Failure of caregivers to utilize such distancing strategies, for example, correlates with lower levels of cognitive development, especially in communication-handicapped children.

Feldman and Goldsmith advance the intriguing hypothesis that the highly stimulating cognitive modes of child care occurring in certain families may in fact emerge from a subcultural pattern of family ecology that transcends and passes through several generations. They report on the phenomenon as it appears in a case study of a single musically talented family in which the confluence of biological and subcultural factors and family ecology and personal circumstances has culminated in exceptional talent in Yehudi Menuhin and to a lesser extent in his two sisters.

Fowler assembles a large body of biographical material on the lives of twenty-five historically outstanding mathematicians, eighteen men and nearly all of the historically known great women mathematicians, to evaluate the intellectual quality of their early life experiences. While evidence is sparse in certain cases, the general pattern is one of highly exceptional and systematic immersion in abstract symbol modes of cognitive processing, typically beginning in the preschool years and quite often during early infancy. Of special interest is the evidence that mathematicians may not always be exposed specifically to mathematical codes early in life, suggesting that early extensive experience in abstract language codes of any kind may later transfer readily to mathematical modes of processing.

Peak outlines how the Suzuki method of infant-child musical training in violin and piano appears to be the creation of a specific culture that may not always be easily transferrable to other cultures. She documents how pervasive the patterns are in Japanese institutions to develop self-regulation in a social context of stringent group forms and values, beginning in earliest childhood, but reinforced at every phase of development in institutions throughout society.

While methodological problems are numerous in these studies— three of them consist of case studies of one form or another, and the others utilize varying combinations of correlation and experimental manipulation—all add valuable information to our still small body of information on how early experience may influence the development of competence, both in the short- and long-term spans of development. All to some degree indicate that early experience may have effects that persist in development over time, but that the effects are not immutable, they are likely to vary with the quality and type of early experience, and they probably must be undergirded by later cultural and ecological support and conditions of continuing stimulation. However, the importance of early stimulation strategies for the generation of high levels of symbol processing, which in turn lead to later highly self-directed modes of learning and problem solving and the continuing development of competence, emerges as a theme in several of the chapters, as in Sigel's distancing strategy, Hunt's high language-coping infants, and the extraordinary self-propelled systems of independent study among the child prodigies in music and mathematics reported by Feldman and Goldsmith, and by Fowler.

William Fowler
Editor

References

Baltes, P. B., and Reese, H. W. "The Life-Span Perspective in Developmental Psychology." In M. H. Bornstein and M. E. Lamb (Eds.), *Developmental Psychology: An Advanced Textbook.*" Hillsdale, N.J.: Erlbaum, 1984.

Bloom, B. S. (Ed.). *Developing Talent in Young People.* New York: Ballantine, 1985.

Brainerd, C. J. "Cognitive Development and Concept Learning: An Interpretive Review." *Psychological Bulletin,* 1977, *84,* 919-939.

Bryant, P. *Perception and Understanding in Young Children.* London: Methuen, 1974.

Casler, L. "Maternal Deprivation: A Critical Review of the Literature." *Monographs of the Society for Research in Child Development,* 1961, *26,* (entire serial No. 80).

Consortium for Longitudinal Studies, The. *As the Twig Is Bent: Lasting Effects of Pre-School Programs.* Hillsdale, N.J.: Erlbaum, 1983.

Davidson, H. P. "An Experimental Study of Bright, Average, and Dull Children at the Four-Year Mental Level." *Genetic Psychology Monographs,* 1931, *9,* 119-289.

Dawe, H. C. "A Study of the Effect of an Educational Program upon Language Development and Related Mental Functions in Young Children." *Journal of Experimental Education,* 1942, *11,* 200-209.

Denenberg, V., and Bell, R. W. "Critical Periods for the Effects of Infantile Experience on Adult Learning." *Science,* 1960, *131,* 227-228.

Feldman, D. H. *Beyond Universals in Cognitive Development.* Norwood, N.J.: Ablex, 1980.

Fowler, W. "Cognitive Learning in Infancy and Early Childhood." *Psychological Bulletin,* 1962a, *59,* 116-152.

Fowler, W. "Teaching a Two-Year-Old to Read: An Experiment in Early Childhood Learning." *Genetic Psychological Monographs,* 1962b, *66,* 181-283.

Fowler, W. *Potentials of Childhood.* Vol. 1, *A Historical View of Early Experience.* Vol. 2., *Studies in Early Developmental Learning.* Lexington, Mass.: Lexington Books, 1983.

Gardner, H. *Frames of Mind: The Theory of Multiple Intelligences.* New York: Basic Books, 1983.

Gelman, R., and Gallistel, C. R. *The Child's Understanding of Number.* Cambridge, Mass.: Harvard University Press, 1978.

Haith, M. M., and Campos, J. J. (Eds.). *Handbook of Child Psychology.* (4th ed.) (P. H. Mussen, Ed.) Vol. 2, *Infancy and Developmental Psychobiology.* New York: Wiley, 1983.

Hebb, D. O. *The Organization of Behavior.* New York: Wiley, 1949.

Hunt, J. M. *Intelligence and Experience.* New York: Ronald Press, 1961.

Jersild, A. T., and Bienstock, S. F. "The Influence of Training on the Vocal Ability of Three-Year-Old Children." *Child Development,* 1931, *2,* 272-291.

Jersild, A. T., and Bienstock, S. F. "A Study of the Development of Children's Ability to Sing." *Journal of Educational Psychology,* 1934, *25,* 481-503.

McGraw, M. *Growth: A Study of Johnny and Jimmy.* New York: Appleton-Century-Crofts, 1935.

McGraw, M. "Later Development of Children Specially Trained During Infancy: Johnny and Jimmy at School Age." *Child Development,* 1939, *10,* 1-19.

Montessori, M. *The Absorbent Mind.* New York: Holt, Rinehart & Winston, 1967.

Orlansky, H. "Infant Care and Personality." *Psychological Bulletin,* 1949, *46,* 1-48.

Palmer, F. H., and Andersen, L. W. "Long-Term Gains from Early Intervention."
In E. Zigler and J. Valentine (Eds.), *Project Head Start: A Legacy of the War on
Poverty*. New York: Free Press, 1979.

Plato. In E. Hamilton and H. Cairns (Eds.). *Collected Dialogues*. Bollingen Series,
no. 71. N.J.: Princeton University Press, 1980.

Raymont, T. A. *A History of the Education of Young Children*. London: Longmans, Green, 1937.

Razel, M. "A Reanalysis of the Evidence for the Genetic Nature of Early Motor
Development." In I. E. Sigel (Ed.) *Advances in Applied Developmental Psychology*. Vol. 1. Norwood, N. J.: Ablex, 1985.

Scott, J. P. (Ed.). *Critical Periods*. Stroudsburg, Pa.: Dowden, Hutchinson & Ross,
1978.

Siegel, L. S., and Brainerd, C. J. *Alternatives to Piaget*. New Yorkk: Academic
Press, 1978.

Watson, J. B. *Behaviorism*. Chicago: University of Chicago Press, 1957.

Yarrow, L. J. "Maternal Deprivation: Toward an Empirical and Conceptual Re-
evaluation." *Psychological Bulletin*, 1961, *58*, 459–490.

Zigler, E., and Valentine, J. (Eds.). *Project Head Start: A Legacy of the War on
Poverty*. New York: Free Press, 1979.

*William Fowler, for many years a professor of applied
psychology at the Ontario Institute for Studies in education
at the University of Toronto, is now a visiting research scientist
in the Eliot-Pearson Department of Child Study at Tufts
University and director of the Center for Early Child Care and
Learning in Cambridge. His interests include the study of early
experience, socialization, day care, and cognitive development.*

The social realities of contemporary society, combined with an extensive body of day-care research, call for recognition by professionals and the public of the need for developing high-quality professional child-care systems necessary to meet the needs of young children and to support family life.

Day Care and Early Environmental Adequacy

Bettye M. Caldwell

A growth-fostering environment for young children may be described quite succinctly as one in which the needs of children can be met. These needs can be described in simple language. Children need families that care for them, shelter them, love and protect them, nurture them, and help them acquire the skills and attitudes that enable them to be reasonably healthy and happy during childhood and to function later as competent adults. They also need a society that backs up its families, one that demonstrates a collective will to support and assist families in the conduct of their child-rearing task. At issue is the question of whether today's environments, in which children spend significant portions of time, are capable of meeting those needs and, if not, how we can facilitate the kinds of changes necessary to ensure that they do.

In this chapter I shall examine some of the social realities that have produced inevitable changes in the environments for child-rearing today. Second, I shall raise questions about the adequacy of the public and professional conceptualization of society's answer—the child-care system—to

An earlier version of this chapter was presented at the MacAuthur Conference on Growth-Fostering Environments for Young Children, Chicago, Illinois, November 29, 1982.

W. Fowler (Ed.). *Early Experience and the Development of Competence.*
New Directions for Child Development, no. 32. San Francisco: Jossey-Bass, June 1986.   **11**

these changes. Third, I shall examine briefly the data base available for making an enlightened decision about whether day care can meet young children's needs. Finally, I shall offer a few suggestions as to ways of improving quality in child care through further research and professional activities and through the formulation of more enlightened social policies pertaining to children and families.

Social Realities and Child-Rearing

Throughout recorded history, the major child-rearing functions during the early years of life have been assigned to the family unit. As is now documented in a wealth of ethnographic reports (see Werner, 1979), there is considerable diversity in the way that assignment is handled, in the specific roles given to different family members, and even in who may and may not be designated as part of the family. Likewise, the values associated with different terminal (that is, adult) behaviors and the techniques used to achieve those behaviors will vary widely from one culture to another. Nonetheless, every society has its own acceptable norms about what constitutes an acceptable family unit and how it will perform its child-rearing tasks. Ours is no exception.

We have generally assumed that the family consists of a father, a mother, and one or more children. We have also assumed that it may include one or more additional adults from the previous or present generation with blood ties to one of the parents—that is, it may be an extended rather than a nuclear family. If all these principal characters in the family unit are present, and if societal resources and circumstances allow physical needs to be met, we have assumed that the family, whether nuclear or extended, can meet the psychological needs of the children who become part of the unit. Although historical descriptions of severe punishment, abandonment, mutilation, and other atrocities (see Rosenheim, 1973) carried out under the banner of family rights might occasionally make us wonder, the family unit has by and large been a workable construct.

What is at question is whether, if the cast of the family unit changes, or if people in the cast choose to play roles that differ from what contemporary Western society considers traditional, the needs of children can still be met. For example, if there is no father available both to produce income and to participate in the socialization of the children, how will the children be affected? And if the mother works outside the home as well as in it, how will this affect the style of child-rearing to which the children are exposed? Or what happens if the cast changes frequently, with one person playing the role of father or mother for a time and then leaving, with or without another person immediately available as a replacement? Such changes are commonplace in today's world (U.S. Bureau of the Census, 1982). For example, consider the following statistics:

1. Over half (54 percent) of all mothers with children under eighteen years of age are in the labor force. Nearly half (48 percent) with children under five are in the labor force.

2. Fewer than one third of children whose mothers work full-time are cared for in their own homes.

3. Approximately 70 percent of children whose mothers work full-time are not cared for by a relative.

4. Roughly one in three new marriages will end in divorce within five years.

5. One out of every five American children lives in poverty; with that figure being one out of two for black children and one out of three for Hispanic children.

6. More than twelve million children (20 percent) live with their mothers only; for blacks this is 50 percent of the children.

7. Approximately one child out of five is born to an unmarried woman.

Such demographics have produced alarm reactions about family life and have raised questions about whether the family environment is one in which the needs of young children can be met. New data (Wallerstein and Kelly, 1979; Hetherington and others, 1978) from studies of the effects of divorce on children are showing more negative sequelae than had long been presumed to exist. Child abuse is often referred to as "a national disgrace," with estimates of the number of children abused each year ranging up to one million. Sexual abuse, a subcategory of child abuse, also has an alarmingly high incidence, with over 90 percent of the alleged offenders being relatives or close friends (estimates provided by the National Committee for the Prevention of Child Abuse). Thus, in many ways it is possible that the family is not the setting for fulfillment and tranquility that it is sometimes represented to be.

These demographics have also produced an intensification of interest in supplementary child care—that is, an arrangement in which part of the child-rearing function is assumed by someone other than primary family members. Because of the demographic changes, supplementary child care has become both more necessary and more visible. This new visibility has led to the same sort of question that is being asked about the family—namely, can the needs of young children be met in such environments?

It is good that both questions should be asked, although each implies a certain misunderstanding of past and present social realities. To raise the question about the family in the face of contemporary social demographics disregards the fact that, during most or all historical periods in most parts of the world, someone other than the mother has provided a substantial amount of care for young children (Aries, 1962). To raise the question about extra-family child care represents a misunderstanding of the extent to which such care is a basic and necessary component of the child-rearing system, and it fails to see the potential of such care to augment family life in significant ways.

Child Care as a Component of the Child-Rearing System

In view of the family and societal realities described earlier, supplementary child care is currently needed for approximately half of the young children in this country. By the end of the century, such care will be necessary for almost all of our young children. This means that a significant part of the socialization of children will take place in professional child-care settings. A major task of the child-care staff will be to reinforce behaviors compatible with social goals the parents have for their children and to encourage behaviors that represent the norms of the broader culture. Thus, child care is actually a subsystem of the broader child-rearing system—and the subsystem outside the family that is likely to be the first to reach the child and to have more hours and days of influence than any of the other (with the possible exception of the mass media, namely, television).

In spite of the importance of extra-family child care for the socialization of children, and in spite of the fact that most children will come into contact with the system for a significant amount of time during their early formative years, the service does not appear to be held in high esteem by the general public. Tocsins are frequently sounded about adverse consequences associated with enrollment of a child, particularly one younger than three years old, in child care of any type. Recent exposés of sexual abuse in such settings have caused general public alarm. Workers in the field receive piteously low salaries and perceive themselves as having little recognition as professionals who make important contributions to the welfare of children and to the well-being of families.

The failure of the public to appreciate the importance of supplementary child care as a vital component of the child-rearing system is an unfortunate consequence of the modern history of child care in America and of the lack of conceptual clarity found in either the language of professional and scientific writing or of everyday conversational descriptions of the service. For example, it is often thought of as a service only for poor children, even poor children from multiproblem families. For many years, use of the service by middle-class mothers somehow stigmatized the families and made the parents feel guilty. It was described as "substitute care," implying that children who experienced such environments were effectively cut off from the natural family environment. Even more pejorative terms such as *institutional* and *custodial* care were used to create images of either abandonment or serious deprivation. Great pains were taken to contrast day care with early education (the nursery school and early educational intervention research), which, although functionally similar except for duration of immersion of the child in the experience, was assumed to have entirely different effects on the participating children. Day care was indicted as not only weakening the basic ties of the children to their families but also as weakening the total family structure. And then the destructive epithet was hurled at day care during the early 1970s that it represented "communal care," and any service so described had to be unpatriotic and un-American.

Most of the components of the public (and scientific) conception of day care are quite inaccurate. Since the rebirth of concern with early experience in the 1960s, there has been ample time for a more accurate concept to emerge. Prior to presenting data pertaining to the impact of day care as a significant early experience in the lives of children, I should like to offer a description of the service that corrects many of the misconceptions referred to above.

Professional child care is a comprehensive service to children and families that supplements the care children receive from their own families. It is in no way a substitute for such care or a competitor for the role of parents in the upbringing of their children. Virtually all children are reared primarily in their own homes by their own families, and virtually all children receive some degree of supplemental care from persons other than their parents.

The need for professional child care will vary quantitatively as a function of demographic characteristics of the family. Families in which the primary caregiver works outside the home as well as inside it because of economic need or choice, or families in which the major caregiver has a disability that interferes with child-rearing, will need relatively more supplementary care. Families in which there are two parents and clear role differentiation relative to income production and household services may need and utilize the professional child-care system only intermittently. Nonetheless, rare indeed would be the family that never needed or used the system of supplementary care in some form.

Professional child-care programs can and do vary in quality, just as family experiences do. Quality will vary as a function of the characteristics and training of the people who provide the service, the physical setting in which it is provided, and the support for such services provided by the society at large. Regardless of whether families need to participate in the subsystem of professional child care to a small or large extent, all families need and are entitled to services of high quality. It is possible to identify those factors associated with quality and to advocate for their availability and the removal or improvement of services that do not possess attributes of quality.

Just as the child-rearing system must be concerned with all aspects of a child's development, so must any service that is part of that system deal with the whole child. Thus, professional child care must foster the development of the child physically, intellectually, and socioemotionally. Such services must have as an overall goal the creation of a growth-fostering environment for young children. In this task there must be close coordination with the children's parents in terms of developmental goals and strategies by which these goals are achieved. Input from representatives of all disciplines concerned with child development is essential if comprehensive programs representing high quality in all components of the service are to be available.

Differences in types of services needed by children from different family settings are more a matter of degree than kind. Those who design and provide professional child-care services have a responsibility to provide a continuum of high-quality services that will appropriately match the needs of children and their families.

Meeting Children's Needs in Child Care

Having now exorcised some of the historical misconceptions about child care and having proposed a more inclusive and accurate contemporary concept, I will consider the question of the adequacy of day care as an early experience for children. Here I will review the evidence briefly in three main areas of development: health and physical development, cognitive development, and socioemotional development. As a number of comprehensive reviews have appeared in the last few years (see Belsky and Steinberg, 1978; Rutter, 1981; Caldwell and Freyer, 1982), I shall only summarize the major findings.

Health and Physical Development. When the first infant-care projects began in the 1960s, there was a great deal of legitimate concern about whether infants could be safely brought together in groups. By that time successful immunization against both polio and measles was possible, thus removing the spectre of epidemics of such dread communicable diseases. Early health research was thus more concerned with whether the annoying but seldom life-threatening illnesses—colds, ear infections, diarrhea, and so on—would show an increase in group programs. Loda, Glezen, and Clyde (1972) studied thirty-nine children ranging in age from one month to five years and found the rate of respiratory illnesses in day-care children similar to that in children of similar backgrounds who did not have the day-care experience. There was a slight but insignificant tendency for children younger than twelve months to have more colds (approximately one more per year). Golden and Rosenbluth (1978) reported similar findings for the New York City Infant Day-Care Study. This research team also noted that health records, maintenance of immunization schedules, and follow-up on health problems were more adequate for children in group than in family day care.

A series of studies by Chang and co-workers in California has examined health-care practices in various types of child-care programs (Chang and others, 1978, 1980; Chang, 1979). The investigators were interested in the types of health personnel available either as staff members or as consultants, the admission policies for mildly ill and handicapped children, and the extent to which child-care workers knew about and used other agency services for additional training and upgrading of practices. Almost all the centers had procedures for referral of acute medical problems and emergency procedures, and about two-thirds had someone designated health coordinator. In the family day-care homes, there was less attention to health matters such as immunization records and information about present or past illnesses. In general the family day-care mothers were isolated from and knew little about other community health programs. In many of the programs, recording of information was inadequate.

Within the past several years there has been an increase in concern about the role of attendance in day care in the spread of Hepatitis A. Hadler and others (1980) conducted a ten-month study of viral hepatitis in Maricopa County, Arizona. Cases were found in about 9 percent of the 308 centers in the county, with the majority of cases occurring in household contacts of the children. Fifteen percent of the cases were employees in the centers. Awareness of this problem has led to increased vigilance of persons responsible for training child-care workers in sanitation practices (particularly the necessity for careful hand-washing with germicidal solution after every cleaning of a child and after every handling of a soiled diaper) and has alerted licensing workers to check more carefully for practices in this area.

Cognitive Development. There has been considerable research dedicated to determining whether child-care programs—especially group care—can favorably influence cognitive development in children. One of the major goals of the experimental infant programs established during the 1960s was to create environmental conditions for learning that could help circumvent the gradual decline in cognitive functioning often observed in disadvantaged children over the first five years of life. In spite of that objective, it was difficult if not impossible to create the kinds of conditions—random assignment of subjects to experimental and control groups, blind evaluations, and so on—considered necessary for exemplary scientific research.

Particularly difficult to achieve was evidence of comparability of groups, in that families that chose to enroll their children in child care could well have differed on a number of variables from families that did not make this choice. For example, if the research population was a disadvantaged poverty group, one might legitimately suspect that there could be important differences in child-rearing conditions available to a group whose mothers had the initiative to work (and therefore needed child care) and a group whose mothers were willing to accept welfare support. If the sample was middle class, having one or more children in day care meant that the mothers were willing to disregard social sanctions against working when one has young children, again identifying them as different in potentially significant ways from a control group. The early research conditions were not unlike those generally prevailing in clinical research situations. There were always a few notable exceptions, however (Ramey and Campbell, 1977), and over time sophisticated researchers have found ways of improving methodology.

In the early 1960s, three historically important infant day-care projects were begun: one in New York state (Syracuse) and two in North Carolina (Chapel Hill and Greensboro). As these were the three projects most closely scrutinized by funding agencies, professional groups, and advocacy groups alike, it is appropriate to cite some of the early results of these projects. Although the projects were begun at about the same time, they all had unique "personalities" and quite different samples: The Syracuse sample was a heterogeneous array of mainly disadvantaged children, some from almost unreal conditions of social pathology; the Chapel Hill sample was clearly bimodal, with almost equal numbers of socially disadvantaged and privileged children; and the Greensboro sample was clearly middle class and served mostly intact professional families.

Early data from the Syracuse project (Caldwell and Smith, 1970) showed significant differences in change scores (Cattell Infant Intelligence and Stanford-Binet Intelligence scores) in the child-care and control samples, with the child-care children showing significantly higher gains. Another interesting finding was that the distributions of scores were "normalized" over time in the experimental children. Early data from the Chapel Hill project were similar. Robinson and Robinson (1971) reported significant differences between children who had entered their program either as young infants or around age two and two groups of controls on a variety of cognitive and language measures. Differences in favor of the experimental children were evident at as early as eighteen months of age, with greatest impact shown in the area of verbal development. Although the widest differences were found in the most disadvantaged children in the two groups, the Chapel Hill group found spectacular gains in some of the middle-class children in their program, causing the Robinsons to speculate that they had not begun to understand the extent to which what was considered normative cognitive development had been dampened by the general accessibility of only a bland and not a truly stimulating developmental environment.

Early results from the Greensboro project (Keister, 1970), with its homogenously middle-class sample, were somewhat different but equally reassuring. Evaluation of the children on a number of cognitive measures revealed essentially no differences between the day-care and control children, leading Keister to the conclusion that for middle-class infants, there were no deleterious effects associated with spending a significant portion of time in infant day care.

Although the methodology of subsequent studies has improved, data from these three early programs are still relevant. These were pivotal projects in the history of child care in America, and their early findings were crucial in helping to turn the tide of professional, if not public, resistance to the idea that development could be fostered in supplementary child-care programs. With somewhat more brevity, albeit more respect and admiration for the way in which design problems were often overcome, I will cite other more recent research that has further enriched and refined our knowledge about cognitive effects associated with early child care.

In a major study done in the Boston area, Kagan, Kearsley, and Zelazo (1977) found results similar to those from the Greensboro project—namely, surprisingly few differences between working- and middle-class Chinese-American and Caucasian children enrolled in an infant-care project and carefully matched controls. The child-care sample functioned slightly better than the controls on nonlanguage items from the Bayley, but there were no other cognitive differences of any magnitude. When the child-care and control groups were pooled, there were major differences associated with class and ethnicity, leading the investigators to conclude that these variables were far more important than whether young children spend part of their time in an extra-family environment.

Certainly one of the most important child-care research projects in recent years has been the Abecedarian Project (Ramey and Campbell, 1977, 1979). Also located in Chapel Hill, North Carolina (which has surely spawned more creative research in child care than any other city, small or large, in the country), the project was elegantly conceived and has been meticulously conducted. Disadvantaged families with infants at high risk for mental retardation were randomly assigned to a longitudinal study group or an intensive child-care group, and several waves of children and parents were carefully followed for long periods with very low attrition rates. Data from these groups have supported both theoretical formulations pertaining to the cumulative impact of an inadequate environment on the cognitive development of young children and on the likelihood that patterns of development can be enhanced by participation in a stimulating extra-family environment. Children in both groups had average Bayley quotients at six months of age. However, children in the longitudinal study group showed a steady decline, while mean scores for the enrichment children remained right around the average level for their age group. At forty-two months the experimental children were still superior to the controls on the McCarthy Scale of Children's Abilities in the verbal, perceptual-performance, quantitative, and memory scales.

There is not time here to try to review all the exciting research data on cognitive effects associated with child care or with different types of child care (family versus group). For a recent summary, one might refer to Caldwell and Freyer (1982). Suffice it to say that there is no need to fear cognitive declines in young children who participate in quality child-care programs.

Socioemotional Development. Although some people were apprehensive about health risks in child care and suspected that cognitive decline might occur, there seemed to be legions who were convinced that children would suffer severe emotional trauma in such settings. In particular, there was concern about whether young children spending long hours most days in the company of adults other than their parents could develop a normal attachment to their own parents, especially their mothers (see Bowlby, 1952). Thus, the effects of early child care on the attachment of children to their mothers has been the major socioemotional variable examined in recent research.

Child Care and Attachment. A study from the Syracuse group (Caldwell and others, 1970) was the first one that dealt with this question, and the findings of the study were largely negative—that is, there were no major differences in attachment patterns at the age of thirty months between children who had been in group infant care from around a year and a reasonably well-matched control group. Attachment was assessed by means of ratings based on a combination of interview and observation. A few years later Blehar (1974) published what would become a landmark study, using the Ainsworth Strange Situation Test (Ainsworth and Wittig, 1969) as the measure of attachment. Subjects were middle-class children from largely intact families (a group quite different from the Syracuse sample). Blehar reported that the younger children (age thirty months) who had been in day care showed anxious-avoidant attachments to their mothers and that the older day-care children (forty months) were prone to show anxious-ambivalent attachment. This study spawned a series of replications and modifications (Moskowitz and others, 1977; Portnoy and Simmons, 1978; Roopnarine and Lamb, 1978), none of which supported Blehar's conclusions that maternal attachment was impaired by early child-care experience.

A study by Blanchard and Main (1979) dealing with this question is worth special mention, in that it added a touch of ecological relevance to the procedure. Although the Strange Situation Test has a touch of experimental splendor, it bears no resemblance to the type of separation children ordinarily experience in child care. Accordingly, these investigators added to the laboratory procedure a direct observation of how the children actually separated from their parents when brought to their child-care centers and how they reacted on reunion. Avoidance of the mother in either setting was unrelated to age or number of hours per week in attendance; however, it was negatively correlated with length of time in child care. The longer the infants were in child care, the better their social adjustment and the less likely they were to show resistance or avoidance on reunion. Furthermore, the amount of avoidance shown by the children was comparable to that shown by children in other published studies who had not had the group experience. Similar findings were reported by Ragozin (1980), who also used naturalistic methods. Thus, as is always the case, findings are dependent on the methodology used by the investigators. However, regardless of method, the sheer weight of numbers is on the side of the interpretation that attachment to the mother is in no way impaired by quality child care.

Child Care and Aggression. Another area of special concern within the socioemotional domain has been aggression. About a decade ago Schwarz, Strickland, and Krolick (1974) reported that a group of three- to five-year-old children who had been enrolled as infants in the Syracuse Children's Center were less task-oriented in the new program and more aggressive than the children who entered after age three. However, their aggression was more likely to be directed toward the newly enrolled children than toward their long-term companions. In fact, the early enrollees were described as often nurturant toward the other children in their subgroup. One design problem in that study was that the groups were not really well matched in that the children who had been in the infant center came from family settings with significantly more social pathology than the late enrolling controls.

A more recent study by Finkelstein (1982) is of more direct relevance to the question of whether child care per se, not age of enrollment, is associated with more aggressiveness. Studying children from the Abecedarian Project (Ramey and others, 1977) after they were enrolled in a public kindergarten, he noted more aggressiveness (hitting, threatening, insulting, and taking things from another child) during recess in the former child-care children than in other kindergarten children who had not had such an experience. In fact, the ratio of incidence of aggression was fifteen to one for the two groups. After evaluating possible reasons for this discrepancy, including the way aggressive behavior had been handled in the daily program, the Abecedarian staff designed a special procedure for handling such behavior in subsequent waves of children enrolled in the program. This involved changing the physical environment and staff training specifically to enhance social skills of young children. After the children had experienced this training program, the incidence of aggressive behavior dropped sharply and did not differ from that of a control group of low-income children who had not been enrolled in child care. Thus, the question of whether there is more aggression in children who have participated in child care, especially from an early age, relates to the conditions of care. It remains an important area for further research.

Program Quality and Developmental Outcomes. Most of the research cited thus far simply looks for associations between day care and some developmental attribute; the investigators often provided little or no information about the level of quality that characterized the programs from which research subjects were drawn. One of the more noteworthy trends in recent years has been research that is not based on simple between-group analyses (groups with and without extra-family child-care experience) but that allows program characteristics to vary and examines developmental outcomes associated with different patterns. The best known of such studies is the National Day-Care Study (Ruopp and others, 1979), which collected data from sixty-four centers in Atlanta, Detroit, and Seattle. Some eighteen hundred children were observed and tested, over one thousand parents interviewed, and caregivers in 129 classrooms were observed and interviewed. Of particular concern were the quality indicators of staff-to-child ratio, small group size, and staff trained in areas related to early education and child development. The variable of group size seemed especially important as a quality indicator in programs for infants, resulting in a recommendation of no more than eight children per group for children under two and no greater than twelve for children in the two- to three-year age range.

A more recent study by McCartney (1984) assessed quality in nine child-care centers in Bermuda by means of the Harms and Clifford (1980) Early Childhood Environment Rating Scale and, in addition, obtained observational measures of the quantity of verbal interaction between caregivers and the children. The children were given several tests of cognitive and language functioning. Quality of the child-care program was as predictive of cognitive and language performance as data about the home backgrounds of the children. Language skills were more highly developed in children attending centers with high levels of caregiver speech. Research of this type—looking for outcome variations associated with quality variations—represents a significant step forward in our understanding of the effects of different kinds of child-care programs on young children. It is reassuring that program components chosen to represent quality and arrayed so as to help create a growth-fostering environment for young children who spend part of their time in child care are indeed associated with favorable developmental outcomes. The next logical question then becomes: How can we improve the quality of the child-care environment?

Improving the Child Care Environment

In this final section, I offer several suggestions for improving quality in child care. These fall into two distinct areas—research issues and policy issues—and are discussed in that order.

Research Issues. Undoubtedly there are many contributions that research can make to improving the child-care environment. I shall mention three that I consider to be most important.

Identifying Potentially Beneficial Components of the Child-Care Experience. Over the past twenty years, research in child care has generally been conducted from a negative orientation—trying to prove that young children are not harmed through a child-care experience. Certainly, in the

Syracuse project our scientific and theoretical hypothesis was that the children would benefit from their experiences in the children's center, but the funding came with a caveat that we must demonstrate that the children were not damaged as a result of the intervention (Caldwell and Richmond, 1964, 1968). As we move into new research areas and work with improved designs, it might be helpful to try to derive from developmental theory and previous empirical findings hypotheses as to areas in which early child care should be associated with developmental advantages.

One of the most obvious examples of an appropriate hypothesis of this nature can be drawn from the influential work of Harlow and his colleagues (Harlow and Harlow, 1966) and students. There is probably no animal experimentation of this century that has had more impact on our ideas about some of the types of behavior appropriate for caregivers of young children. Wire and cloth mothers and what they could and could not do to reassure and earn the "love" of infant monkeys have had a major impact on what we train (or encourage) caregivers to do with infants and young children. But there was another concept derived from data collected in the Wisconsin Primate Laboratory that somehow never made the papers or became part of our everyday vocabulary: the peer affectional system. Somehow that term is just not as sensational as wire and cloth mothers.

In the writings of Harlow and Harlow (1966), there was some equivocation about whether the peer affectional system was as important as or more important than the maternal affectional system. Most typically the Harlows describe these two systems as complementary and interactive, implying that both are important for development. Daily play sessions with peers helped to rehabilitate infants subjected to inadequate maternal surrogates. (I have heard Harry Harlow say in lectures that a Rhesus monkey could grow up to be "normal" if it had a lousy mother but an opportunity for play with peers, but not vice versa. I am not certain that he ever stated this quite so definitively in writing, however.) My point here is that, for whatever reasons, we have neglected this aspect of the influential Harlowian theory in our child-care research. Many of the children in our child-care programs experience turbulent family situations. Does participation in child care—involvement in the peer affectional system—help these children adjust to family instability and conflict? In reviewing the literature, I could find only one paper that dealt with this topic (Mehl and Peterson, 1981), and that was a case study reporting spontaneous peer therapy in a child-care setting. Yet here is a clear example of a theory-based empirical question that should be uniquely amenable to child-care research.

There are possibly other such examples that should be a challenge to researchers. For example, does early participation in a social setting enable children to take on the role of the other at an earlier age? Can early participation in social groups lead to more altruism and cooperation in children? Are the suggestions of more aggressive behavior in children who have been in child care related to progression through the peer affectional system and not to a developmental end point? Child-care programs provide a rich field setting for the investigation of such issues.

Improving Quality of Research Designs. It is just as legitimate to talk about improving the quality of research in child care as it is to demand that the quality of available child care be improved. The tremendous upsurge in child-care research during the past decade represents an important beginning. However, much of it has dealt with a fairly narrow range of questions and has employed only marginally adequate research methodology. True experimental designs are almost nonexistent, in that random sampling in between-group comparisons is rarely feasible. And even with reasonably careful matching on relevant moderator variables, there may well be important differences that determine group membership.

In addition to design problems relating to appropriate controls, much child-care research has lacked ecological validity (Bronfenbrenner, 1979). This has been especially true in the large number of studies concerned with attachment. The Strange Situation Test, until it had been applied in child-care research, had primarily been used with infants and toddlers. Older children would inevitably have a totally different set of memories through which to filter the experience of being left alone in a strange room (out of which mother walks, without so much as an "I'll be right back,") on a day when her child probably assumed that they were going on an outing together!

In addition to the above methodological problems, child-care research has been entirely too oriented to outcomes—albeit temporary outcomes—and has neglected process research. Except for a few notable exceptions (Rubenstein and Howes, 1979; Honig and others, 1970; Cochran, 1977), little research effort has been devoted to the important task of describing what goes on in different kinds of child-care programs. Until we know more about what actually takes place, except as can be deduced from a hypothetical daily program filed with a licensing agency, we will have little basis for formulating and testing hypotheses about types of child behavior associated with patterns of input.

Determining Long-Term Effects. This is one of the most pressing research issues and one to which professionals in the field are now ready to respond. All of the outcome research cited earlier has dealt with the effects of certain types of child-care experiences after very short periods of time in the programs; virtually nothing is known about long-term effects. And yet, if child care is a significant aspect of the child-rearing system, how can such effects be trivial? If they are, then perhaps we have overestimated the impact of such programs. If they are not, then we cannot afford not to know what they are.

There can be little question but that the long-term follow-ups reported by the Consortium for Longitudinal Studies (Lazar and Darlington, 1982)) and by Schweinhart and Weikart (1980) have had a major impact on policy makers. It is important to note that within the guidelines of the integrative definition of child care that I offered earlier, these studies represent long-term follow-ups of children who have been in child care. But none of the programs included in the consortium were the long-day programs about which many people are concerned. Furthermore, all of them were programs of high quality in so far as we knew how to define quality at the time the intervention programs were conducted. We need this same kind of follow-up across time and across different patterns of subsequent experience in order to feel confident that quality child care can indeed be a growth-fostering experience. In some of its formats, it *does* provide group socialization at an earlier age than has been normative for our culture. Over time, does this make children more or less sensitive to peer pressure? Does it make them less or more tolerant of group experience? Does the earlier exposure to values that might compete with family values produce more intra-family conflict? What kinds of family members do such children make after they are grown? Can they shed one relationship and form a new one more quickly than is considered adaptable? Is their earlier enrollment in school-type settings likely to be associated with early drop-out or burn-out?

Such questions are constantly being raised by critics of child care, and they deserve serious research attention. We cannot afford to wait to allow definitive answers to emerge from newly constituted, prospective longitudinal studies; early approximations of understanding will have to come from retrospective analyses of available information on the life experiences of children who, during their early years, participated in different kinds of child-care programs.

Policy Issues. Most scientists, either voluntarily or involuntarily, have matured to the point of understanding that research is not enough when sensitive social issues are involved; somehow the knowledge base must be woven into the political process before constructive action can occur. In this final section I shall identify three important issues to which our attention should be given in order to help formulate an enlightened social policy about growth-fostering environments for young children that can embrace the child-care environment.

Informing the Public. As documented in a recent article (Caldwell, 1983), the child-care field has been the victim of an incredibly bad press. Some of this has resulted from the writings of irresponsible journalists (for example, Browning, 1982); sometimes it has taken the form of a sensational headline for an otherwise relatively factual article. Occasionally it has come from highly respected professionals who in public statements do not apply the same rigor of verification that they might demand of their own scientific data. An example is the assertion made a few years ago by a distinguished developmental psychologist, who shall remain unnamed, that day care "would process children like hot dogs." That same scientist later directed a major infant-care project that is widely quoted as showing no aversive effects and relatively few discernible differences among samples with some and with no extra-family child care.

The bad press received by the child-care profession probably reflects attitudes of fear about the service that lurk just below the surface in the minds of many people, professionals, and laypeople alike. Any instance of malfeasance thus gets blown out of proportion, as though to justify these underlying negative attitudes. For example, an instance of child abuse in a professional child-care setting—terrible and inexcusable though it may be—is allowed to obscure the statistic that child abuse, physical and sexual, occurs overwhelmingly in the home at the hands of close relatives or friends.

Several national organizations have recognized this need for a more accurate understanding of child care by the general public, and they have begun to explore ways of helping to raise the public's consciousness about the field.

Any public information campaign has to be approached with consummate care, for it is as easy to be glibly reassuring as it is to be glibly accusatory. If, for example, we chose to characterize the many studies that demonstrate no deleterious effects associated with child care as indicating that the experience did not make a great deal of difference in the lives of children, we could be setting the field up for onslaughts against quality. "After all," might come the countercharge, "if the differences are so slight, why are training, adult-to-child ratio, group size, and so on so important? We might as well choose the cheapest child-care program." As pointed out earlier, quality indicators *are* important, and it is essential to get that information across in any public information campaign.

Defining and Achieving Quality. *Quality* is one of the shibboleths we have used in the in-group in recent years, with most of us feeling that we know what we are talking about but somehow evading the difficult task of specifying exactly what we mean by the term. The National Association for the Education of Young Children has recently launched an accreditation system. This will allow child-care centers that strive for quality—that work to achieve more than the minimal standards generally endorsed in state licensing statutes—to go through a process that will result in either the identification of areas of weakness in the program, for which technical assistance may be arranged, or the awarding of a certificate indicating that the center represents quality as defined by the standards on which the accreditation is based. Having such a procedure in place will help day-care administrators realize that, if they are to be considered professional, they have to assume the major responsibility for self-monitoring of quality—carefully screening potential staff members to make certain that latent abusers or inadequately trained persons are not hired for this important work. Professional responsibility also means keeping abreast of research findings regarding child outcomes associated with different educational procedures, being aware of health risks and knowing how to minimize them, and knowing about and using effective management techniques. Once this accreditation procedure becomes operational, its sheer existence will serve as a motivator to child-care personnel. The certificate it offers should provide a hallmark of quality to parents and to other professional groups concerned with the welfare of young children.

Ensuring an Interdisciplinary Base. The child-care field has grown up essentially between the cracks of other human service fields. Now various disciplines are clamoring to possess child care as their own without always showing the necessary recognition of the importance of other fields. Obviously early childhood education is a major discipline—even though for many years leaders in this field refused to allow day care into the fold. Such services have no chance of offering quality without a strong health component and without social service ties. Developmental psychologists also ignored the field for many years but have now become interested. It is to be hoped that they will bring with them a more sophisticated approach to evaluation than has heretofore characterized the field. The educational link must also embrace elementary schools, as vertical linkages are as important as horizontal ones.

There are other linkages needed by the child-care field. Certainly business and industry need to be aware of the needs of families for this service and to feel that they have a responsibility to make a contribution to it. This is true not only in terms of having industry help subsidize the service but also in terms of recognition of the field as an example par excellence of a small business operation and as an area therefore worthy of training and technical assistance. Legal aspects of child care are complex and perhaps poorly understood by many persons in the field. All other professional groups will undoubtedly come to give more consideration to the role they have to play in the conceptualization, the implementation, and the monitoring of child care as the level of public consciousness rises about the importance of the field to children and families.

Conclusion

The major child-rearing objective of the adults in any society is to create the sort of environment for young children in which the children's needs can be met. In Western culture we have tended to operate on the assumption that those needs can be met only in an environment in which an infant has the exclusive custody of her or his mother on an ad lib, full-time basis. The demographics of family life reveal the fact that such environments, if indeed they ever existed, are in the minority in today's world.

28

Accordingly, it is mandatory that researchers concerned with the effects of early experience examine the potential of day care either to facilitate or to inhibit development in young children.

Research on the effects of day care has generally shown that young children's health, socioemotional, and cognitive development progresses at least as well in professionally-run group care as it does when children are cared for entirely at home. Programs may vary considerably, however, and research on day care programs indicates potential for improvement in quality and the need to focus more on specific dimensions of day care. Among measures suggested in this chapter to improve quality in infant child care are to define day care as a child-care system run by professionals to supplement care in the home and to establish general standards among providers to include licensing and professional responsibility. If such actions are taken, it is suggested that day care can indeed provide a growth-fostering environment for young children.

References

Ainsworth, M. D. S., and Wittig, B. A. "Attachment and Exploratory Behavior of One-Year-Olds in a Strange Situation." In B. M. Foss (Ed.), *Determinants of Infant Behavior*. Vol. 4. London: Methuen, 1969.

Aries, P. *Centuries of Childhood: A Social History of Family Life*. New York: Knopf, 1962.

Belsky, J., and Steinberg, L. D. "The Effects of Day Care: A Critical Review." *Child Development*, 1978, *49*, 929-949.

Blanchard, M., and Main, M. "Avoidance of the Attachment Figure and Social-Emotional Adjustment in Day-Care Infants." *Developmental Psychology*, 1979, *15*, 445-446.

Blehar, M. C. "Anxious Attachment and Defensive Reactions Associated with Day Care." *Child Development*, 1974, *45*, 683-692.

Bowlby, J. *Maternal Care and Mental Health*. Monograph Series, no. 2. Geneva: World Health Organization, 1952.

Bronfenbrenner, U. *The Ecology of Human Development*. Cambridge, Mass.: Harvard University Press, 1979.

Browning, D. "Waiting for Mommy." *Texas Monthly*, February 1982.

Caldwell, B. M. "How Can We Educate the American Public About the Child Care Profession?" *Young Children*, 1983, *38*, 11-17.

Caldwell, B. M., and Freyer, M. "Day Care and Early Education." In B. Spodek (Ed.), *Handbook of Research in Early Childhood Education*. New York: Free Press, 1982.

Caldwell, B. M., and Richmond, J. B. "Programmed Day Care for the Very Young Child: A Preliminary Report." *Journal of Marriage and the Family*, 1964, *26*, 481-488.

Caldwell, B. M., and Richmond, J. B. "The Children's Center—A Microcosmic Health, Education, and Welfare Unit." In L. Dittman (Ed.), *Early Child Care: The New Perspectives*. New York: Atherton Press, 1968.

Caldwell, B. M., and Smith, L. E. "Day Care for the Very Young—Prime Opportunity for Primary Prevention." *American Journal of Public Health*, 1970, *60*, 690-697.

Caldwell, B. M., and others. "Infant Day Care and Attachment." *American Journal of Orthopsychiatry,* 1970, *60,* 690-697.

Chang, A. "Health Services in Licensed Family Day Care Homes." *American Journal of Public Health,* 1979, *69,* 603-604.

Chang, A., Zuckerman, S., and Wallace, H. M. "Health Services Needs of Children in Day Care Centers." *American Journal of Public Health,* 1978, *68,* 373-377.

Chang, A., and others. "Health Services in Infant Day Care Centers." *Child Care Quarterly,* 1980, *9,* 51-58.

Cochran, M. M. "A Comparison of Group Day and Family Childrearing Patterns in Sweden." *Child Development,* 1977, *48,* 702-707.

Finkelstein, N. W. "Aggression: Is It Stimulated by Day Care?" *Young Children,* 1982, *37,* 3-9.

Golden, M., and Rosenbluth, L. *The New York City Infant Day-Care Study.* New York: Medical and Health Research Association of New York City, Inc., 1978.

Hadler, S. C., and others. "Hepatitis A in Day-Care Centers." *The New England Journal of Medicine,* 1980, *302,* 1222-1227.

Harlow, H., and Harlow, M. "Learning to Love." *American Scientist,* 1966, *54,* 244-272.

Harms, T., and Clifford, R. M. *Early Childhood Environment Rating Scale.* New York: Teachers College Press, 1980.

Hetherington, E. M., Cox, M., and Cox, R. "The Aftermath of Divorce." In J. H. Stevens, Jr., and M. Matthews (Eds.), *Mother-Child/Father-Child Relationships.* Washington, D.C.: National Association for the Education of Young Children, 1978.

Honig, A. S., Caldwell, B. M., and Tannenbaum, J. "Patterns of Information Processing Used by and with Young Children in a Nursery School Setting." *Child Development,* 1970, *41,* 1045-1065.

Kagan, J., Kearsley, R. B., and Zelazo, P. R. "The Effects of Infant Day Care on Psychological Development." *Evaluation Quarterly,* 1977, *1,* 109-142.

Keister, M. E. *A Demonstration Project: Group Care of Infants and Toddlers.* Final report submitted to the Children's Bureau, Office of Child Development, U.S. Department of Health, Education, and Welfare, June 1970.

Lazar, I., and Darlington, R. B. "Lasting Effects of Early Education: A Report from the Consortium for Longitudinal Studies." *Monographs of the Society for Research in Child Development,* 1982, *47,* (entire serial no. 195).

Loda, F. A., Glezen, W. P., and Clyde, W. A., Jr. "Respiratory Disease in Group Day Care." *Pediatrics,* 1972, *49,* 428-437.

McCartney, K. "Effect of Quality of Day-Care Environment on Children's Language Development." *Developmental Psychology,* 1984, *20,* 244-260.

Mehl, L. E., and Peterson, G. H. "Spontaneous Peer Psychotherapy in a Day-Care Setting: A Case Report." *American Journal of Orthopsychiatry,* 1981, *51,* 346-350.

Moskowitz, D. S., Schwarz, J. C., and Corsini, D. A. "Initiating Day Care at Three Years of Age: Effects on Attachment." *Child Development,* 1977, *48,* 1271-1276.

Portnoy, F., and Simmons, C. "Day Care and Attachment." *Child Development,* 1978, *49,* 239-242.

Ragozin, A. S. "Attachment Behavior of Day-Care Children: Naturalistic and Laboratory Observations." *Child Development,* 1980, *51,* 409-415.

Ramey, C. T., and Campbell, F. A. "The Prevention of Developmental Retardation in High-Risk Children." In P. Mittler (Ed.), *Research into Practice in Mental Retardation.* Vol. 1: *Care and Intervention.* Baltimore, Md.: University Park Press, 1977.

Ramey, C. T., and Campbell, F. A. "Early Childhood Education for Psychosocially Disadvantaged Children: Effects on Psychological Processes." *American Journal of Mental Deficiency*, 1979, *83*, 645–648.

Ramey, C. T., and others. "An Introduction to the Carolina Abecedarian Project." In B. M. Caldwell and D. J. Stedman (Eds.), *Infant Education for Handicapped Children*. New York: Walker, 1977.

Robinson, H. B., and Robinson, N. M. "Longitudinal Development of Very Young Children in a Comprehensive Day-Care Program: The First Two Years." *Child Development*, 1971, *42*, 1673–1683.

Roopnarine, J., and Lamb, M. "The Effects of Day Care on Attachment and Exploratory Behavior in a Strange Situation." *Merrill-Palmer Quarterly*, 1978, *24*, 85–95.

Rosenheim, M. K. "The Child and the Law." In B. M. Caldwell and H. Ricciuti (Eds.), *Review of Child Development Research*, Vol. 3. Chicago: University of Chicago Press, 1973.

Rubenstein, J. L., and Howes, C. "Caregiving and Infant Behavior in Day Care and in Homes." *Developmental Psychology*, 1979, *15*, 1–24.

Ruopp, R., and others. *Children at the Center. Final Report of the National Day-Care Study*. Vol. 1. Cambridge, Mass.: Abt Associates, 1979.

Rutter, M. "Social-Emotional Consequences of Day Care for Preschool Children." *American Journal of Orthopsychiatry*, 1981, *51*, 4–28.

Schwarz, J. C., Strickland, R. G., and Krolick, G. "Infant Day Care: Behavioral Effects at Preschool Age." *Developmental Psychology*, 1974, *10*, 502–506.

Schweinhart, L. J., and Weikart, D. P. "Young Children Grow Up: The Effects of the Perry Preschool Program on Youths Through Age 15." *Monographs of the High/Scope Educational Research Foundation*. Ypsilanti, Mich.: High/Scope Press, 1980.

U.S. Bureau of the Census. *Trends in Child-Care Arrangements of Working Mothers*. Current Population Reports, Series P-23, nos. 117 and 129. Washington, D.C.: U.S. Government Printing Office, 1982.

Wallerstein, J., and Kelly, J. "Children and Divorce: A Review." *Social Work*, 1979, *24*, 468–475.

Werner, E. E. *Cross-Cultural Child Development*. Monterey, Calif.: Brooks/Cole Publishing Company, 1979.

Bettye M. Caldwell is Donaghey Distinguished Professor of Education at the University of Arkansas at Little Rock. She has been a leader in program development and research in the field of infant day care for over twenty years. One of her concerns has been the concept of the day-care environment as an important type of early experience influencing development.

*Variations in the quality and type of infant care in institutional
and other settings in different cultures and social classes can
have profound influences with important implications for
long-term development on the child's rate, level, and type of
cognitive development.*

The Effect of Variations in Quality and Type of Early Child Care on Development

J. McVicker Hunt

In his book *The Children's Cause*, Steiner (1976) credits or discredits—
depending on your point of view—Bloom (1964) and Hunt (1961) with
convincing Robert E. Cooke, Professor of Pediatrics at Johns Hopkins
University Medical School, and through him John Fitzgerald Kennedy
and Sargent Shriver, that "there already exists adequate understanding of
the problems and processes involved to permit an immediate and massive
intervention in the poverty cycle [because poverty-stricken children lack]
the kinds of experiences and opportunities which are available to more
economically advantaged familes" (p. 27). This statement was made in
Dr. Cooke's letter to Sargent Shriver. Steiner also notes that the unusual
influence of these books on political policy was an accidental consequence
of the sensitivity to mental retardation in these political leaders resulting
from the fact that the president and Mrs. Shriver had a mentally deficient
sister. Also, they had chosen as their pediatrician Dr. Robert Cooke, who
himself had a mentally deficient son.

Many of us closest and most knowledgeable about the role of early
experience were highly ambivalent about the launching of Project Head
Start. I believed then and I still believe that most of the problems children

W. Fowler (Ed.). *Early Experience and the Development of Competence.*
New Directions for Child Development, no. 32. San Francisco: Jossey-Bass, June 1986.

of poorly educated, poverty-stricken parents commonly have in school result from a lack of the kinds of experiences and opportunities that are typically available in more economically and educationally advantaged families. However, I did not then and do not now feel that "there already exists adequate understanding of the problems and processes involved to permit an immediate massive intervention in the poverty cycle."

Following World War II, evidences of plasticity in behavioral development, and especially in early behavioral development, accumulated rapidly. It was this evidence that Bloom and I reviewed. This evidence suggested that if the role of early experience in early psychological development were more fully understood, "it might be possible to increase the average level of intelligence within the population substantially. . . . There would, of course, be a long step between learning how to effect changes in child-rearing and getting them adopted by the culture, but learning how is the first step" (Hunt, 1961, p. 346).

Although we were excited by the prospect of public support for early education, we recognized that it is one thing to have evidence that a goal is attainable, but something very different to have the technology for achieving that goal. Moreover, we feared that overselling such a broad-scale program as Project Head Start might well lead to unrealistic expectations that children of poorly educated, poverty-stricken parents would achieve the academic levels of children from the educated middle class with only a summer or a year of schooling to make up for four years of experience of poor development-fostering quality.

Project Head Start did indeed fail to achieve this highly unrealistic goal. In fact, Project Head Start achieved less in the way of academically related gains than the compensatory early education carried out under the auspices of universities. As Payne and others (1973) note, Head Start programs failed to draw from current professional knowledge, paraprofessionals were inadequately trained and supervised to aid teaching, and transportation services were poorly organized—resulting from the grass-roots belief system with which they were run.

Nevertheless, it is unfair to accept the commonly made assertion that Project Head Start failed, first, because it was the commitment and excitement of Head Start that led to the professional demonstrations of compensatory education by Caldwell (1968), the Deutsches, Cynthia and Martin (see Gotkin, 1968), Gray and Klaus (1965), Nimnicht, McAfee, and Meier (1969), Weikart (1969), Hughes, Wetzel, and Henderson (1968), and others. Second, although all of these demonstrated that the children of poorly educated, poverty-stricken parents could learn when exposed to experiences of the improved development-fostering quality prescribed, their rate of development relapsed relative to that of children from middle-class homes as soon as they became solely dependent on their families and the public schools for development-fostering, quality experience. Third, whenever compensatory education was begun at age three or earlier, rather than at age four, the resulting gains were usually greater, as would be expected from the principle that plasticity decreases with age. Fourth, the efforts of Levenstein (1970, 1976) in fostering children's intellectual and motivational development through a program of providing toys and teaching caseworkers how to encourage mothers to engage in conversation with their children between one and two years of age showed a great deal of success that persisted to first grade.

Her success and Karnes and others' (1970) success in a similar intervention program encouraged me to believe a better way of attacking the problem would be to teach the parents how to foster the intellectual and motivational development of their children beginning at birth. The program planned was very small-scale, and it was concerned with determining how much the rate of early psychological development can be modified and what kinds of experience are most effective in facilitating intellectual and motivational development.

The challenge became clear while I was writing *Intelligence and Experience* (Hunt, 1961). In reviewing the literature, it became evident that the psychometric approach to intelligence that began in the anthropometric laboratory of Francis Galton was based on a belief in hereditary determinism, which was part of the Zeitgeist of the nineteenth century. The sensorimotor tests that Galton devised, apparently for a eugenic purpose, were too simple to show a correlational relationship with teachers' estimates of intelligence (Bolton, 1891) or school grades (Wissler, 1901), as Binet and Henri (1895) pointed out. Believing that the "fundamental faculty" of intelligence consists of judgment, good sense, initiative, and adaptability, Binet and Simon (1905) constructed tests involving knowledge that turned out to provide scores that showed substantial correlation with the criterion variables of Bolton and Wissler.

It is highly ironic that Binet (1909, p. 54), who deplored "the verdict that the intelligence of an individual is a fixed quantity," probably did as much to perpetuate that view as anyone. When he and Simon sought a single metric with which to represent intelligence, because they took it to be a unitary faculty, they achieved that single metric by means of substitutive averaging to obtain the mental age. They also, thereby, permitted the same mental age to represent a variety of intellectual attainments. When Stern (1912) saw the necessity of dividing a child's mental age by her or his chronological age, the resulting intelligence quotient (IQ) fit so well with the dominant prevailing hypothesis of hereditary determinism that it came to be considered a constant assessment of genotypic intellectual potential rather than what it is, namely, a summary measure of past phenotypic attainments. When this model for psychometric testing was employed to measure early psychological development, this averaging so obscured the role of experience in the psychological development of infancy and the later preschool years that corrective evidence, which should have been discerned long ago, went largely unnoticed and disregarded.

Piaget's (1951, 1952, 1954) observations of the early psychological development in his own three children made it clear, at least to me, that several branches of sensorimotor development exist and that what he termed *stages* are probably sequential landmarks of transformation in the structural organization of these branches. It seemed likely, therefore, that one might construct ordinal scales with which to measure separately these separate branches.

I was exceedingly fortunate to have Ina Uzgiris as a collaborator on this project. We identified seven branches of sensorimotor development and constructed an ordinal scale for each one. They are (1) visual following and object permanence, (2) the development of means for obtaining desired environmental events, (3) vocal imitation, (4) gestural imitation, (5) operational causality, (6) object relations in space, and (7) schemes for relating to objects (Uzgiris and Hunt, 1966, 1975). She, more than I, was responsible for the work that went into our ordinal scales.

I viewed these scales mainly as a means of investigating, first, the degree to which the ages infants attain these behavioral landmarks of transition is modifiable by experience, and, second, the hypothesis that a relationship exists between kinds of experience and kinds of developmental advance. For the first question, the model that my collaborators and I used was the range of reaction (first demonstrated by Woltereck, 1909, with self-fertilizing daphia), that is, the amount by which genetic potentials (for the same population) can vary in phenotypic expression as a result of experience. By using as an analogue of the range of reaction the most extremely different mean ages of attaining the top steps on these scales—using samples of infants from different populations as well as differing rearing conditions—we have admittedly taken a methodological liberty that weakens somewhat the import of this evidence. For the latter question, we took evidence of a relationship between kinds of experience and kinds of development wherever we found it because Gesell (1954), in emphasizing the determining role of heredity in psychological development, claimed that "the child always reacts as an integer" (p. 339). In his sound cinema *Life Begins,* Gesell was even more explicit in saying that "maturation proceeds apace along all systems simultaneously." With this as the dominant prevailing view, all evidence between kinds of experience and kinds of development becomes important theoretical exceptions that justify utilizing such evidence where it is found.

The evidence that I report here derives from several sources. The first of these was a cross-sectional study done by Paraskevopoulos and myself in Athens, Greece, which compared the means and standard deviations of the ages of three groups of children, being reared under very different circumstances, who were at the top level on four of our scales, namely, object permanence, development of means, gestural imitation, and vocal imitation. The three differing sets of rearing conditions consisted of those at the Municipal Orphanage, where the infant-caregiver ratio was approximately 30-to-3 (or 10-to-1); the Metera Center, where the infant caregiver ratio was only 3-to-1, and the caregivers were both trained and carefully supervised; and the sample of ninety-four home-reared children of working-class families who were examined at the day-care center utilized while their mothers worked (Paraskevopoulos and Hunt, 1971).

The second was a longitudinal study of the effects of an educational day-care program on the first eight consecutive children born to the poorly educated, poverty-stricken parents served by the Mt. Carmel Parent and Child Center in Illinois (see Hunt, 1980). The third was the program of longitudinal studies of samples of foundlings without detectable pathology, who were taken from the Municipal Orphanage of Tehran, at what was considered to be more than four weeks of age, to the orphanage of the Queen Farah Pahlavi Charity Society, where they received a series of development-fostering enrichments (Hunt and others, 1976). This ten-year program (1966–1975) employed five consecutive samples, here termed *waves*, of foundlings whose selection for waves was essentially random. The first wave of fifteen foundlings served as controls, and the only intervention consisted of being examined with the ordinal scales every other week during their first year and every fourth week thereafter until they were transferred from this orphanage for nurslings to another for walking children at an average of 169 weeks of age.

The second wave of ten foundlings received an abortive attempt at audiovisual enrichment, due to failure to maintain equipment and complete the program. The third wave of ten foundlings received untutored human enrichment that consisted merely of reducing the infant-caregiver ratio from about 30-to-3 to 10-to-3, thereby allowing the caregivers to spend more time with their charges. The fourth wave of twenty foundlings received a proper administration of the *audiovisual* enrichment, with tape recordings of music and mother-talk and mobiles, all contingent on infant activation. By this time it was discovered that none of the controls and none of those who received the abortive attempt at audiovisual enrichment had acquired any evidence of language, receptive or expressive, by the time of their transfer to the orphanage for walking children. For this reason, the focus of treatment for the fifth wave was shifted from intrinsic motivation to language acquisition, and the caregivers were taught how to facilitate the development of vocal imitation as a means of fostering language acquisition. Thus, the foundlings in the fifth wave received what we termed *tutored human enrichment*.

Results

The Cross-Sectional Study in Athens. Because obtaining findings from longitudinal studies is inevitably very time-consuming, the cross-sectional study in Athens, where my collaborator, John Paraskevopoulos, knew of these orphanages with widely different programs of child-rearing, was done in order to demonstrate the likely value of a more expensive series of longitudinal studies. The mean ages of the children at the next-to-top level on the scales of object permanence, vocal imitation, and gestural imitation were dramatically different. Those at the Municipal Orphanage who had attained the top level on the scale of object permanence had a mean age of 197 weeks (3 years, 9.33 months). Those at Metera Center who had attained the top step of object permanence had a mean age of 154.94 weeks (2 years, 11 months). Thus, the saving was of the order of 10 months or 21 percent. Those home-reared who had attained the top level of object permanence had the youngest mean age of 131.07 weeks (2 years, 6 months, and 1 week). Thus, they averaged 1 year and 4 weeks younger than those at the Municipal Orphanage. The top step on this scale of object permanence consists of retrieving a desired object that has disappeared into a container after the container itself has disappeared under three successive covers, with the child going first to the last cover under which the container disappeared and proceeding backward until finding it.

For the scale of vocal imitation, none of the sixty-seven children examined at the Municipal Orphanage had attained either of the top two steps, even though many of them were already 5 years old. Of the fifty-two children examined at the Metera Center, only four had achieved the top level. Of the ninety-three home-reared children, however, twenty-three had achieved the top level and their mean age was 151 weeks (just short of three years). Thus, even though the failure of any child at the Municipal Orphanage to attain the top two steps makes it impossible to specify differences in mean ages of attainment, the fact that none of the children at the Municipal Orphanage had attained it at less than three years of age suggests that retardation in vocal imitation was even greater than that of object permanence. Moreover, together, these two findings from the cross-sectional study clearly justified the expense of a longitudinal study.

For gestural imitation, however, twenty-six of the sixty-seven children at the Municipal Orphanage had attained the top level at a mean age of 132 weeks, and nearly half of those at Metera Center had achieved the top level at a mean age of 114 weeks. Of the home-reared infants, forty-one of the ninety-three had achieved the top level at the mean age of 108 weeks. Thus, orphanage experience appears to be more deleterious for the development of object permanence and for vocal imitation than for gestural imitation. Where the difference between the means of the ages of the Municipal Orphanage and home-reared children who had attained the top level of object permanence was 66 weeks, the difference between the mean ages of these same two groups at the top level of gestural imitation was only 24 weeks. Although it is impossible to state such a discrepancy in mean ages for those at the top level for vocal imitation, it is probably even greater than that for object permanence, and definitely greater than that for gestural imitation. Once this fact was discerned, it became clear that vocal and gestural imitation should not be regarded as one system. It takes but minimal analysis to note that gestural imitation is dependent on visual motor experience, while vocal imitation must come via auditory-vocal experience. Thus, vocal imitation demands considerable experience of vocal interaction, which is largely absent in orphanage-rearing because caregivers seldom talk to or with their charges.

The variance in the ages of these three groups of children who had attained the top level differed to a surprising degree. It was hardly surprising that the standard deviation (34.37) of those at the Municipal Orphanage who were at the top level of object permanence was of the order of twice that (17.36) for the children of Metera Center. When no more than three caregivers were in charge of thirty infants, it was inevitable that some children came to be favored while others were neglected. In contrast, at Metera Center, where each caregiver had but three infants in her charge, and the caregivers were both trained and supervised, the development-fostering quality of experience must have been comparatively well standardized, and at some better level. What was surprising was finding that the standard deviation of the home-reared children from working-class families who had attained this top level of object permanence was 47.22 weeks, or 13 weeks larger than that for the Municipal Orphanage children at this same level. Apparently the development-fostering quality of experience provided in working-class families varies even more than that at the Municipal Orphanage.

The Evaluative Study of Educational Day Care at the Mt. Carmel Parent and Child Center. At the time of this evaluative study, the focus of the Badger learning program was on teaching the caregivers to keep the infants provided with things of high interest to them. In retrospect, the thing most interesting to them had been a shape-sorting box produced by Creative Playthings. It consisted of a box with five holes in a hinged top. The shapes of these holes and the corresponding blocks were round, square, rectangular, isoceles triangular, and irregular triangular. When these infants played with this toy, the blocks disappeared but were readily retrieved for further play merely by lifting the hinged lid, which made the blocks visible and accessible for grasping once more. This device was well designed to furnish the sort of disappearing-reappearing experiences that appear to foster the development of object permanence.

This experience resulted in the youngest mean age (73 weeks) for attaining the top step on the scale of object permanence that we have encountered. The oldest mean age is that attained at the Municipal Orphanage in Athens. Although the mean age of those children *at the top level* was 197 weeks, we have estimated that the mean age of attainment was of the order of 184 weeks by halving the difference between the mean ages of those at the top level (197 weeks) and those at the next-to-top level (171 weeks). Thus the difference between the highest and lowest mean ages of attainment (184 weeks and 73 weeks) is 111 weeks, or 2 years and 7 weeks. This result of the retardation from orphanage-rearing, combined with the effect of the educational day care employing the shape box at Mt. Carmel, represents the best estimate that we have of the range of reaction for the age of attaining the top step on this scale of object permanence. The difference of 111 weeks represents a saving of a little over 60 percent in age of attainment. Transformed to IQ ratios for this particular landmark in object construction, this difference is on the order of ninety points.

For the scale of vocal imitation, our estimate of the range of reaction is less satisfactory. Because all or a majority of children reared at both the Municipal Orphanage in Athens and the Orphanage of the Queen Farah Pahlavi Charity Society failed to achieve the top step of vocal imitation before they were transferred to the orphanage for walking children, and no instructions to continue the examining there were issued, we have no ages for attaining the top steps. Hunt and others (1976) used the mean age of transfer, but this clearly yields an underestimation of the actual mean age of attainment. Even so, we are inclined to believe that the range of reaction was as large or larger for vocal imitation than the one we obtained for the scale of object permanence.

Yet this contention should be verified because the development of vocal imitation appears to be of a special importance in the development of the symbolic processes. This is implied in the following finding: The children from poorly educated, poverty-stricken parents served by the Mt. Carmel Parent and Child Center generally attained the top steps ahead of the 12 home-reared children from predominantly middle-class families in Worcester, Massachusetts. They attained the top steps on three of the four scales employed for the evaluation of that early form of the Badger Infant and Toddler Learning Programs. They were ahead by 25 weeks, on the average, in attaining the top step on the scale of object permanence, ahead by 22 weeks in attaining the top step on the scale for the development of means, and ahead by 11.41 weeks for gestural imitation. But they were 20 *weeks behind* the Worcester children in attaining the top step on the scale of vocal imitation. Since the average of the mean ages of attaining the top steps on the four scales was 85.04 weeks for the Mt. Carmel children with the help of the educational day care, but 94.57 weeks for the home-reared children of predominantly middle-class families in Worcester (a saving of slightly more than 10 percent in favor of the Mt. Carmel children) we fully expected the IQs of the Mt. Carmel children to be higher than the IQs for the Worcester children. This expectation was based on the Binet-Simon practice of averaging and on the finding of a correlation of +.87 for performances of older children on a set of Piagetian tasks with Stanford-Binet IQs by Humphreys and Parsons (1979). But the results surprised us.

The IQs of the Worcester children later averaged 111. Yet, when the Mt. Carmel children were approaching their fourth birthdays, my collaborator, Girvin Kirk, examined them with the Stanford-Binet. He returned from his hundred-mile trip with the longest face I have ever seen. While one child, the daughter of a couple who were serving as paraprofessionals at the center, had an IQ of 133, the IQs of the other seven were all between the low 70s and the low 80s.

At first, I was as devastated, too, but when emotion had waned sufficiently to permit thought, this finding began to make theoretical sense. First, a retardation of 20 weeks in the attainment of the top step on the scale of vocal imitation had overbalanced mean advances in three of the four scales, even the advance for object permanence, in predicting the IQ. Second, it is clearly the symbol systems of language and numbers that are essential in information processing. Third, language skills figure heavily in both the content and the administration of the Stanford-Binet test. Thus, finally, vocal imitation must figure strongly in language acquisition, Chomsky's claims (1959) notwithstanding. Language interaction was not a strong component of the early Badger program.

I should also note that again, we encountered larger standard deviations in the ages of attaining the sequences of steps on these four scales by the eight consecutive children born into the poorly educated, poverty-stricken parents served by the Mt. Carmel Parent and Child Center than we did the twelve home-reared children from predominantly middle-class families in Worcester. Moreover, the discrepancy between the standard deviations is largest by far for the scale of vocal imitation, in which the standard deviations for these lower-class infants from the poverty sector range from two to nearly five times those for the Worcester infants from predominantly middle-class families (see Hunt, 1980).

A Comparison of Project Head Start Children and Nursery School Children: Social Class and Language Skill. Our investigations of social class and language skills was prompted by the claims of such sociological students of language as Baratz and Baratz (1970) and Labov (1970) that the language of poverty-stricken children, and especially those who are black, is merely different from standard English, but not inferior for purposes of communication. We began by administering the Peabody Picture Vocabulary Test. Though the mean IQ of three-year-olds at a nursery school for children from well-educated families averaged 111.6, that for three Head Start classes averaged 72.3—a difference of 39.3 points of Peabody IQ. Here again, we encountered quite unexpectedly standard deviations in IQ that were substantially higher for the Head Start children than for the nursery school children. The only difference we found between black and white poor children of Head Start consisted of greater proneness to use the word "black" for the brown block by black children than by white children.

The other parts of this program compared the three-year-olds at

Head Start and nursery school in semantic mastery of such elementary abstractions as color (Kirk, Hunt, and Lieberman, 1975), position (Hunt, Kirk, and Volkmar, 1975), shapes (Hunt, Kirk, and Lieberman, 1975), and numbers (Kirk, Hunt, and Volkmar, 1975). Suffice it to say that between 76 and 82 percent of the nursery school children could name the sample of six colors (red, yellow, green, blue, orange, and brown) without error when blocks of the respective colors were pointed to by the examiner, asking, "What color is this block?" For children of Head Start, the corresponding percentages ranged only between 22 and 25 percent. For receptive mastery, the difference was even greater: 90 percent of the nursery school children could pick out the proper blocks three times in succession when their colors were named by the examiner, but only 19 to 22 percent of the Head Start children could do so. For positions and shapes, the percentages of both groups performing correctly were substantially lower, but those for the nursery school remained from three to four times greater than those for the children of Head Start, and the differences were higher for receptive language than expressive. Contrary to the claims that were made by Baratz and Baratz (1970) and such proponents of nonstandard English as Labov (1970), requiring children to communicate among themselves concerning colors, positions, shapes, and numbers served only to exaggerate the manifestation of their semantic deficiency (Kirk, Hunt, and Volkmar, 1979). Clearly, many children of poorly educated, poverty-stricken parents, whether black or white, suffer from a basic semantic deficiency in the symbolic processing of such information, which must inevitably hamper their ability to profit from schooling. On the other hand, it should be clearly noted that within Project Head Start, race differences, with the one exception already mentioned, were notable for their absence.

Untutored Human Enrichment at the Orphanage of the Queen Farah Pahlavi Charity Society. All the subjects at the Tehran Orphanage were foundlings from the Municipal Orphanage of Tehran, selected at no more than four weeks of age by the director and her pediatric consultant on the basis of absence of any detectable pathology. Both the fifteen foundlings of the control wave and the ten foundlings of the second wave who received the abortive attempt at audiovisual enrichment were slow in sitting alone and in standing and moving about their cribs. The ten foundlings in the second wave did not attain the locomotor landmark of standing and moving until the average age of seventy weeks. When I arrived for my annual planning visit, the foundlings of the third wave, who received the untutored human enrichment, were between eleven and thirteen months of age, yet they were all standing and moving about their cribs. They had achieved this landmark in posture and locomotion at a mean age of forty-one weeks, an advance of twenty-nine weeks on the average in the attainment of this postural locomotor landmark. This was very exciting until I examined the performances of these foundlings on the ordinal scales. At that time, they were all somewhat behind both the controls and those of the second wave who had received the abortive attempt at audiovisual enrichment.

Inquiry soon revealed that the caregivers had used the extra time obtained from the reduced infant-caregiver ratio (from 30-to-3 to 10-to-3) to carry their charges about and to put them in walkers. The former had served to exercise their balancing mechanisms. The latter had invited their use of the stepping schema and of putting weight on their feet and legs. This exemplified a relationship between kinds of experience and kinds of developmental advance, for such experiences had advanced the development of posture and locomotion without in any way facilitating development along the several branches of cognitive development assessed by the Piaget-inspired ordinal scales.

The infants from the fourth wave who had been exposed to a fairly well-implemented program of audiovisual enrichment, but who otherwise received no special attention or improvement in child-care ratios, made substantial gains on all seven scales. They generally surpassed the infants of the third wave in attaining top steps in six of the seven scales, though differences were not significant, despite the fact that third-wave children enjoyed superior child-care ratios (10-to-3 versus 30-to-3). They lagged only in object permanence and in imitating unfamiliar visible gestures. These results suggest potentials for enrichment experiences through mechanical means, particularly when institutions are short-staffed. Tape-recorded music and mother-talk and special mobiles, provided they are at least partially graded in difficulty and contingent on infant activation, can contribute usefully to cognitive development during infancy. This is not to say that mechanical enrichment should ever be considered a substitute for human contact and care.

The Tutored Human Enrichment Program at the Municipal Orphanage of Tehran. When it became clear that neither the first-wave control foundlings nor the second wave foundlings had acquired any sign of language by age 3 (third- and fourth-wave foundlings had acquired very little also), it was decided that the focus of the program for the fifth wave should be shifted from intrinsic motivation to the facilitation of language acquisition. According to a hypothetical scenario for language acquisition, gleaned from the literature and Mt. Carmel-Worcester findings, the phonetic aspect of language is acquired chiefly via vocal imitation. The semantic aspect is acquired through a combination of vocal imitation of the sounds heard in temporal connection with objects felt or seen. And syntax starts when a child makes creative use of her or his semantic attainments in the interest of an attempt to communicate. Yet, it is shaped by a combination of imitation and parental tutelage toward the grammatical rules of the language. Vocal imitation has its own developmental epigenesis (see Uzgiris and Hunt, 1975).

On the basis of this hypothetical scenario, therefore, we taught the caregivers to start by imitating the cooings of their foundlings as soon as they could in order to get vocal games going. We also taught them to watch for a series of infant attainments that would serve as cues for modifying the educational treatment while solving what I have called "the problem of the match" (see Hunt, 1961; Uzgiris and Hunt, 1985).

Once an infant had begun to produce three different vocal patterns, the first attainment cue, the caregivers were to enter into the leadership rather than the mere imitation of the infants' sounds. They were to employ pseudo-imitation in order to start a vocal game with one of the child's existing vocal patterns, play it back and forth, and then shift to another, play it back and forth, shift to another, and so on. Along the way, the caregiver was to shorten the number of interactions with each separate vocal sound as the number of interactions with each separate vocal sound increased. Once their charges could follow directly as the caregiver shifted from one familiar vocal sound to another, the caregiver had a second cue for a change in the educational treatment. At this point, the caregiver was to try modeling phonemes from the Farsi language that she had never heard her charge produce.

As more and more of the interaction involved unfamiliar vocal patterns, and as her infant charge or charges became more and more adept at producing good copies of these unfamiliar phonemes, the caregiver was to watch for the cue for a third change of treatment. This came when her charge could produce good copies of almost any phonemic pattern of no more than two syllables immediately without going through a series of successive approximations. With this cue, the caregiver was to introduce yet another change of experiences designed to facilitate the acquisition of expressive semantic mastery, or the naming of things involved in the caregiving process. Believing that nothing is more palpable than feeling a part of the body touched, my paradigm concerned ear-washing. The caregiver was to say, "Now I am going to wash your *ear*," and as her vocal emphasis came on the word ear, the washcloth was to make contact with the infant's ear; similarly, labeling was timed to coincide with washing other parts of the body, with different forms of attention to pieces of clothing, utensils, and so on. It is this that we called "tutored human enrichment," and with this procedure for facilitating the acquisition of semantics, the special tutelage of the caregivers terminated.

The effects were dramatic. In contrast to the very limited language acquisition of any children in the earlier waves who had reached the age of three, the ten of these fifth-wave foundlings whom I actually saw in my final planning visit (one had been adopted before I arrived), all had vocabularies of fifty or more words for the parts of their bodies, the pieces of the clothing they wore, the tableware, the furniture, and so forth. All of them had been observed to use language in their interactions with each other, but curiously, not with their caregivers who seemed to have limited their vocal interactions with their charges to the imitative vocal games in which they had been instructed.

All ten of these foundlings of the fifth wave had attained the top steps on all seven of the ordinal scales. This was something no other wave of foundlings had achieved before they were moved from the orphanage for nurslings to the one for walkers at 169 weeks of age. The average of the mean ages at which they attained the top steps on these seven scales was 87.71 weeks. This is 5.15 weeks younger than that (92.86 weeks) for the home-reared children from predominantly middle-class families of Worcester. This difference of 5.15 weeks constitutes a saving of only 5.55 percent in the average of the mean ages of attainment of the top steps on all the seven scales. But this is rather remarkable when one considers that these were foundlings from the same population as those in the other waves, and that they were reared in the same orphanage in which a third to all of the foundlings in the other waves had failed to attain the top steps on all of the scales before the move at 169 weeks. Because of this move, we obtained no proper data for comparison.

The next most advanced wave consisted of the ten third-wave foundlings who received the untutored human enrichment. The average of their mean ages for attaining the top steps on the seven scales was 121.43 weeks. Since these mean ages were obtained by using the age of transfer for those foundlings who had failed to attain top steps, they underestimate the actual average of the mean ages of attainment. Even so, the difference of 33.72 weeks between the third-wave and the fifth-wave averages for the seven mean ages of attainment constitutes a saving of approximately 28 percent.

If one uses such data as are available from the home-reared children of Athens and Worcester for the mental-age norm, one can divide this norm by the average of the mean ages of attaining the top steps on these seven scales to tranform them into estimates of mean IQs. The estimated mean IQ for the controls and the foundlings in the second wave is between 65 and 70 points. If the foundlings in those two waves were to remain in the orphanage until they were of school age, their mean IQs would almost certainly drift downward to the average of 50 points found by Dennis (1973) as the mean IQ of the children reared from birth to school age at the Creche in Lebanon. Conversely, if these foundlings of the fifth wave, who received tutored human enrichment, were all adopted by parents characterized by the chief examiner as "very high people," as many of them eventually were, they could be expected to attain IQs in a range from 115 to 120 because the IQs of the Worcester children at school age were over 110. This is the evidence and the reasoning behind my claim that the range of reaction for the IQ is probably of the order of 70 points, or the difference between a low of 50 and a high of 120.

The other effects of the tutored human enrichment received by the foundlings in the fifth wave must be mentioned here. First, the caregivers claimed that they could not have loved these foundlings more if they had been their own children. The caregivers of no other group made any like claims. I was doubtful at first, but after seeing tears in the eyes of one caregiver following an adoption of one of her charges, I decided that the caregivers suffered from genuine separation grief. Although I did not at the time know enough of Ainsworth's work on attachment to utilize her assessment of patterns of attachment (Ainsworth and others, 1978), I did observe on two occasions that when these caregivers arrived in the morning, their charges were waiting for them and were obviously glad to see them, and this all-too-sketchy evidence of secure attachments helps to explain the finding of the second effect.

The second effect concerned the contrast in appearance and in such personality characteristics as trust and initiative between the foundlings of the first two waves, on the one hand, with those who received the "tutored human enrichment," on the other. They were frightened by strange people and they manifested almost no initiative. I have considered these infants human analogues of the dog subjects that could not escape electric shock and as a consequence developed "learned helplessness" in the investigations of Overmier and Seligman (1967), Seligman (1975), and Maier and Seligman (1976). In contrast, the foundlings of the fifth wave, who received the tutored human enrichment, wore happy expressions, came forward to be picked up even by a strange American psychologist, were continually engaged in activities of their own choosing, and yet would wait politely for their turn to get my attention if I was engaged in interaction with someone else. It is no doubt for these reasons that the children from the fifth wave were so readily adopted.

Conclusion

It would appear that variations in early experience, beginning at birth, can make very great differences in intellectual equipment and in such personality characteristics as trust, initiative, and even appearance. The pattern of findings furnishes evidence with respect to several important issues of how variations in early experience influence the development of competence.

Perhaps the most important of these is the regularity with which changes in the quality of early child care altered the rates and levels of intellectual development in children. Improvements in care of any type brought improvements in development in both residential and group day-care settings, and multiple efforts at improvement further enhanced development. Simply improving child-care ratios in institutional settings, for example, which enabled caregivers to devote more attention to fewer infants, made substantial differences in outcomes, as did the addition of mechanical forms of enrichment such as mobiles and tape recordings of music and mother-talk contingent on infant activation. The combination of improving ratios and furnishing special training to caregivers resulted in highly dramatic gains, matching or even surpassing the development of children reared in advantaged middle-class homes.

Also significant is the correspondence between variations in types of cognitive domains of care administered and the patterns of competence acquired. Most notable among the effects of specific types of influence was the effect of attention to the quality of language experience. Improving child-care ratios, furnishing infant contingency-operated tape recordings and mobiles, and training caregivers to provide infants with spatial manipulative toys all resulted in important perceptual-motor cognitive gains; but only training caregivers to focus specifically on language brought large gains in language development. The importance of language for abstract symbolic development appears in the contrast between the large gains in perceptual-motor cognitive gains and the continued low Binet IQ scores (70 to 80) of poor children in day care who were given extensive perceptual motor but little language experience. Variations in the types of perceptual-motor gains also appeared, as was illustrated by the development of postural and locomotor control of infants who had received special experiences of being carried by their caregivers and moving in walkers.

Among important implications of the findings in these collected studies is the possibility of utilizing mechanical devices for furnishing supplementary forms of cognitive enrichment, particularly in understaffed settings, as suggested by the multiple gains in perceptual-motor cognitive skills and language by infants experiencing audiovisual enrichment with tape recordings and mobiles. Complexity grading and infant activation appear to have been important components of this strategy, but it is also noteworthy that gains did not match those of infants under the care of specially trained caregivers under optimal ratio circumstances.

Equal in importance is that the wide range of reaction reflected in the large variation in outcomes resulting from differences in the type and quality of early experience suggests the untapped potential for development from environmental influences. The pattern of outcomes across institutions, cultures, and populations further indicates the potential for cognitive development. The long-term potential for development from enriched early experience is indicated by how quickly prospective parents adopted the orphaned infants given selectively enriched cognitive and language experiences. As was the case in the classical study of Skeels (1966), infants in orphanages given high-quality care, which includes stress on cognitive and language processes, developed a good cognitive foundation that made them desirable for adoption into caring homes that would ensure continued high-quality care for later development. The apparent ease with which modestly educated caregivers from different cultures could be trained to adopt cognitively enriched forms of infant care underscores the potentials for extending such opportunities to children of all classes and cultures.

References

Ainsworth, M. D. S., and others. *Patterns of Attachment.* Hillsdale, N.J.: Erlbaum, 1978.

Baratz, S. B., and Baratz, J. C. "Early Childhood Intervention: The Social Science Base of Institutional Racism." *Harvard Educational Review,* 1970, *40* (1), 29–50.

Binet, A. *Les idées modernes sur les enfants (Modern Concepts of Infancy).* Paris: Ernest Flamarion, 1909, (cited from G. D. Stoddard, "The IQ: Its Ups and Downs." *Educational Record,* 1939, *20,* 44–57).

Binet, A., and Henri, V. "La psychologie individuelle (Psychology of the Individual). *Année Psychologique,* 1895, *2,* 411–463.

Binet, A., and Simon, T. "Méthodes nouvelles pour le diagnostic du niveau intellectuel des anormaux" (New Methods for Diagnosing Abnormal Intelligence). *Année Psychologique,* 1905, *11,* 191–244.

Bloom, B. S. *Stability and Change in Human Characteristics.* New York: Wiley, 1964.

Bolton, T. L. "The Growth of Memory in Schoolchildren." *American Journal of Psychology,* 1891, *4,* 362–380.

Caldwell, B. M. "The Fourth Dimension in Early Childhood Education." In R. D. Hess and R. M. Bear (Eds.), *Early Education.* Chicago: Aldine, 1968.

Chomsky, N. "Review of *Verbal Behavior* by B. F. Skinner." *Language,* 1959, *35,* 26–58.

Dennis, W. *Children of the Creche.* New York: Appleton-Century-Crofts, 1973.

Gesell, A. "The Ontogenesis of Infant Behavior." In L. Carmichael (Ed.), *Manual of Child Psychology.* New York: Wiley, 1954.

Gotkin, L. G. "Programmed Instruction as a Strategy for Developing Curricula for Disadvantaged Children." *Monographs of the Society for Research in Child Development,* 1968, *33* (8), (entire issue 124).

Gray, S. W., and Klaus, R. A. "An Experimental Preschool Program for Culturally Deprived Children." *Child Development,* 1965, *36,* 887–898.

Hughes, M., Wetzel, R. J., and Henderson, R. W. *The Tucson Early Education Model.* Tucson: College of Education, University of Arizona, 1968. (ED 033 753)

Humphreys, L. G., and Parsons, C. K. "Piagetian Tasks Measure Intelligence and Intelligence Tests Assess Cognitive Development." *Intelligence,* 1979, *3,* 369–382.

Hunt, J. M. *Intelligence and Experience.* New York: Ronald Press, 1961.

Hunt, J. M. *Early Psychological Developments and Experience.* Heinz Werner Lecture Series. Worcester, Mass.: Clark University Press, 1980.

Hunt, J. M., Kirk, G. E., and Lieberman, C. "Social Class and Preschool Language Skill: IV. Semantic Mastery of Shapes." *Genetic Psychology Monographs,* 1975, *92,* 115–129.

Hunt, J. M., Kirk, G. E., and Volkmar, F. "Social Class and Preschool Language Skill: V. Cognitive and Semantic Mastery of Number." *Genetic Psychology Monographs,* 1975, *92,* 131–153.

Hunt, J. M., and others. "The Psychological Development of Orphanage-Reared Infants: Interventions with Outcomes (Tehran)." *Genetic Psychology Monographs,* 1976, *94,* 177–226.

Karnes, M. B., and others. "Educational Intervention at Home by Mothers of Disadvantaged Infants." *Child Development,* 1970, *41,* 925–935.

Kirk, G. E., Hunt, J. M., and Lieberman, C. "Social Class and Preschool Language Skill: II. Semantic Mastery of Color Information." *Genetic Psychology Monographs*, 1975, *91*, 299–316.

Kirk, G. E., Hunt, J. M., and Volkmar, F. "Social Class and Preschool Language Skill: III. Semantic Mastery of Position Information." *Genetic Psychology Monographs*, 1975, *91*, 317–337.

Kirk, G. E., Hunt, J. M., and Volkmar, F. "Social Class and Preschool Language Skill: VI. Child-to-Child Communication and Semantic Mastery of the Information in the Message." *Genetic Psychology Monographs*, 1979, *100*, 111–138.

Labov, W. "The Logic of Non-Standard English." In F. Williams (Ed.), *Language and Poverty*. Chicago: Markham, 1970.

Levenstein, P. "Cognitive Growth in Preschoolers Through Verbal Interaction with Mothers." *American Journal of Orthopsychiatry*, 1970, *40* (3), 426–432.

Levenstein, P. "The Mother-Child Home Program." In M. C. Day and R. K. Parker (Eds.), *The Preschool in Action*. (2nd ed.) Boston: Allyn and Bacon, 1976.

Maier, S. F., and Seligman, M. E. P. "Learned Helplessness: Theory and Evidence." *The Journal of Experimental Psychology: General*, 1976, *105*, 3–46.

Nimnicht, G., McAfee, O., and Meier, J. *The New Nursery School*. New York: General Learning Corporation, Early Learning Division, 1969.

Overmier, J. B., and Seligman, M. E. P. "Effects of Inescapable Shock upon Subsequent Escape and Avoidance Learning." *Journal of Comparative and Physiological Psychology*, 1967, *63*, 28–33.

Paraskevopoulos, J. B., and Hunt, J. M. "Object Construction and Imitation Under Differing Conditions of Rearing." *Journal of Genetic Psychology*, 1971, *119*, 301–321.

Payne, J. S., and others. *Head Start: A Tragicomedy with Epilogue*. New York: Behavioral Publications, 1973.

Piaget, J. *Play, Dreams, and Imitation in Childhood*. (C. Gattegno and F. M. Hodgson, Trans.) New York: Norton, 1951.

Piaget, J. *The Origins of Intelligence in Children*. (M. Cook, Trans.) New York: International Universities Press, 1952.

Piaget, J. *The Construction of Reality in the Child*. (M. Cook, Trans.) New York: Basic Books, 1954.

Seligman, M. E. P. *Helplessness*. San Francisco: Freeman, 1975.

Skeels, H. M. "Adult Status of Children with Contrasting Early Life Experiences." *Monographs of the Society for Research in Child Development*, 1961, *31*, (entire serial no. 106).

Steiner, G. *The Children's Cause*. Washington, D.C.: The Brookings Institute, 1976.

Stern, W. *The Psychological Methods of Testing Intelligence*. (G. M. Whipple, Trans.) Baltimore, Md.: Warwick and York, 1912.

Uzgiris, I. C., and Hunt, J. M. "An Instrument for Assessing Infant Psychological Development." Urbana: Psychological Development Laboratory, University of Illinois, 1966. (Mimeographed.)

Uzgiris, I. C., and Hunt, J. M. *Assessment in Infancy: Ordinal Scales of Psychological Development*. Urbana: University of Illinois Press, 1975.

Uzgiris, I. C., and Hunt, J. M. (Eds.). *Infant Performance and Experience: Uses of the Uzgiris-Hunt Ordinal Scales of Infant Psychological Development*. Urbana: University of Illinois Press, 1985.

Weikart, D. P. "Comparative Study of Three Preschool Curricula." Paper presented at the biennial meeting of the Society for Research in Child Development, Santa Monica, Calif., March 1969.

Wissler, C. "The Correlation of Mental and Physical Traits." *Psychological Monographs*, 1901, *3*, (entire serial no. 16).

Woltereck, R. "Weitere experimentelle Untersuchungen uber Artveranderung, spezial Uber das Wesen quantitativer Artunterschiede bei daphniden" (Further experimental inquiry into species changes, particularly on the character of quantitative differences in daphia). *Verhandlungen der Deutschen Zooligschen Geselleschaff*, 1909, *19*, 10-173. (From Dunn, L. C. *A Short History of Genetics.* New York: McGraw-Hill, 1965).

J. McVicker Hunt is professor emeritus of psychology and early education at the University of Illinois and past president of the Eastern Psychological Association and the American Psychological Association. He has received several honorary degrees, won numerous awards from psychological associations, and authored several books, including the classic Intelligence and Experience *(1961), and over two hundred journal articles.*

Early exposure to didactic, authoritative teaching
experiences negatively influences cognitive development.

Early Social Experience and the Development of Representational Competence

Irving E. Sigel

The role early experience plays in subsequent mental development is an old problem in developmental psychology and education. In spite of numerous discussions, however, the issues should be reexplored in the light of recent findings and theory in biogenetics from which new perspectives on the course of cognitive growth have emerged (Harris, 1983; Scarr, 1985). The earlier futile heredity-environment controversy appears to be emerging in a different frame, namely, the degree to which the biogenetic make-up predestines the course of individual mental development (McCall, 1979; Scarr, 1985; Waddington, 1969), essentially a continuation of the "fixed versus malleable" controversy of cognitive growth (Hunt, 1961).

The question is: Is the course of mental developmental universal for the species, with experience contributing to variability in mental com-

The research reported in this chapter was supported in part by the National Institute of Child Health and Human Development Grant No. R01-HD10686 to Educational Testing Service, National Institute of Mental Health Grant No. R01-MH32301 to Educational Testing Service, and Bureau of Education of the Handicapped Grant No. G007902000 to Educational Testing Service.

W. Fowler (Ed.). *Early Experience and the Development of Competence.*
New Directions for Child Development, no. 32. San Francisco: Jossey-Bass, June 1986.

petence predetermined by the biogenetic program? There are still those who will argue that biological make-up forms but a broad spectrum of constraints, and optimizing the experience of the child will significantly alter the course and rate of his or her mental development. Two viewpoints seem to prevail in theories of cognitive development. One is exemplified by Piaget (1950), who argues that there are qualitative and structural changes in the nature of children's development of mental representation. Another view asserts that "the basic conceptual apparatus is in place early in ontogeny and that the nature of mental representation is invariant in its fundamental structure, although it may change in terms of its complexity" (Bullock, 1985, p. 170). Neither of these viewpoints explicitly incorporates the role of experience into its framework. Although Piaget acknowledges the role of *social* experience generally as one of the important factors involved in cognitive development, very little if any of his work directly addresses just how and what types of social experience are important.

Discussions of these viewpoints are found in Harris's (1983) excellent review of infant cognition. He cites evidence that reflects the argument that by nature the human organism is programmed for age-specific cognitive competencies that unfold in a universal, predetermined form. Universality does not preclude variations in rate of expression or quality of performance. Rather, universality defines a basis for development interacting with other genetically and nongenetically influenced characteristics (for example, social, familial, and educational experience).

The assumption that cognitive competences are universal provides the basic argument that is developed in this chapter. In pursuit of evolving a conceptual statement regarding the relationship of early experience to subsequent mental competence, a number of additional issues are addressed that seek a reconciliation of Piagetian concepts of developing cognition with current biogenetic programming. The model presented in the concluding section of this chapter reflects how these themes have guided my family research program.

Basic Propositions of My Research

The propositions underlying my conceptualization reflect the influence of the current thinking in behavioral genetics (Plomin and DeFries, 1980; Scarr, 1985); structural developmental (Piaget, 1950); Kelly's (1955) personal construct theory; Polanyi's (1958) personal knowledge; Weiner's (1967) cybernetics; and Werner's (1978) orthogenetic principle:

1. Humans, by their biogenetic nature, are inherently endowed with the capacity to organize and transform experiences into some form of representation.

2. Humans are active, outreaching organisms, and in their active

outreach engage and simultaneously influence the environment. Through this outreach the individual constructs his or her sense of social and physical reality. These constructs are in effect mental representations of that reality.

3. These constructions typically proceed from a global to an increasingly differentiated, ongoing reorganization. With increasing differentiation and integration, new organizations are generated that provide the basis for adaptations to the ongoing life situation.

4. The developmental changes in organization are in part determined by the individual's social experience, since all humans are embedded in a social matrix, initially a primary-care-giving environment, usually the family. The family environment, while embedded in the culture, often creates its own idiosyncratic environment. In this context varieties of intra-familial experiences interact with biogenetic variables, all of which combine to generate individual differences in intellectual (mental competence), social (attitudinal and value), and personality arenas.

5. The individual engages the environment on many levels. Changes in mental competence occur because the individual is confronted with discrepant experiences that often demand resolution. The resolution is usually achieved by mental reorganizations of experiences into a new and more complete whole.

6. These developmental changes evolve in a stagelike sequence in which feedback provides the stimulation for continued modification, expansion, and placement of the representation of experience into a hierarchy. These transformation processes are possible because of the inherent capacity of the organism to carry out such cognitive functions.

7. The coalescence of the biogenetic nature of the organism and the social interactions yields a construct system (a cognitive structure) that develops its own momentum for guiding further interactions with physical, social, and personal reality and becomes increasingly autonomous yet related to its particular developmental history.

8. The emergent construct system is modifiable within the biogenetic parameters coupled with the nature of the environmental feedback. In addition, the permeability of schema boundaries developed over the life course influences the capability of the individual to assimilate new material and make appropriate accommodations to such new knowledge.

Characteristics of Social Experience
Fostering Representational Competence

Although the terms *representation* and *competence* are recognized in the literature, no markers in the form of process, products, or skills are provided to differentiate representational functions from other cognitive processes. Representation is internalization of experience and subsequent

52

competence in three functions: anticipation, hindsight, and transcendance of the ongoing present. The competence aspect refers to the understanding of the rule that experience can be transformed into various sign and symbol systems and that instances retain a core identity in spite of the transformation. A three-dimensional apple and a picture of an apple, while differing in form and mode of presentation, still retain a common identity. I refer to this as *conservation of meaning;* the meaning is retained in spite of media transformations (Sigel, 1978). Conservation of meaning is a necessary prerequisite for understanding transformation rules.

The specific representational thinking processes are defined as follows: *anticipation*—those mental activities that may be rooted in but are not of the present object world but of the future (planning and predicting); *hindsight*—which encompasses two mental processes, reconstruction of past events (short or long term) and reorganization of those past experiences in the service of re-presenting events in the transcendence; and finally, *transcendence* of the ongoing present—those processes that involve reflective abstraction (Piaget, 1978) or transforming ongoing experience into symbolic or sign systems and understanding the transformation rules relevant to this process. These processes function in interrelated ways, for example, deriving from past experience, but they can be isolated and measured. Although the ability to represent is universal, the understanding of the transformation rules will vary as a consequence of social experience. Social experiences that foster or generate discrepancies set the context for the development of representational thinking. The relevant social behaviors that create discrepancies and require representational thinking for their resolution are referred to as distancing strategies, since they are cognitive demands for the child to separate himself or herself cognitively from the immediate behavioral environment to cope with the instigated discrepancy: "Distancing is a way to characterize differentiation of the subjective from the objective, the self from others, ideas from actions. Representational competence is hypothesized as the resultant of experiences creating such distance" (Sigel, 1970, p. 113).

Levels of Distancing Strategies

Distancing strategies vary in level of demands placed on the child by others (see Table 1). A large number of strategies have been identified by observing parents, teachers, and peer interactions. The array was reduced to three levels defined in terms of the cognitive-demand quality of the strategy.

Distancing strategies, while usually verbal, can also be expressed nonverbally by manipulating the physical environment, removing objects—changing spatial configuration in rooms, for example. In sum, any set of actions that creates discrepancies through cognitive demands

**Table 1. Mental Operational Demands (MOD) on the Child
Through Parent Distancing Strategies**

High-Level Distancing	Medium-Level Distancing	Low-Level Distancing
evaluate consequence	sequence	label
evaluate competence	reproduce[a]	produce information
evaluate affect	describe similarities	describe, define
evaluate effort and/or performance	describe differences	describe— interpretation
evaluate necessary and/or sufficient	infer similarities	demonstrate
infer cause-effect	infer differences	observe
infer affect	symmetrical classifying	
infer effect	estimating	
generalize	assymmetrical classifying	
transform	enumerating	
plan	synthesizing within classifying	
confirmation of a plan		
conclude		
propose alternatives		
resolve conflict		

Note: Three main groupings will be used on the level of the distancing demand on the child.
[a]Reproduce/—— (another MOD)—These will be grouped according to the MOD, ignoring the reproduction aspect. Example: reproduce/lab—Low MOD; reproduce/plan—High MOD.

instigates representational thinking. (Although affect is intrinsically involved in the situation and plays an important role in influencing the child's coping with the discrepant event, it will not be developed in this chapter. See Sigel, 1985, for a detailed discussion of cognition and affect.)

Distancing strategies are considered significant for the development of representational competence as a function of their form, level of cognitive demand, and match to the child's developmental level (age alone is not the relevant factor defining distancing behavior). Thus, when the strategy is in an inquiry form, making high-level cognitive demands appropriate to the child's cognitive level, the child is able to respond in a relevant way. If the inquiry is at too low a level, it does not create a discrepancy, and the response is routine or minimally reflective. When the inquiry is beyond the child's comprehension level, the child can only respond at his or her level (that is, impose an idiosyncratic interpretation) and avoid involvement. It is experiences of these types, when appropriately calibrated with the child's developmental level, that provide the bases for developing representational competence.

Prototypes of anticipation, reconstruction, and transcendence of the immediate environment are evident in the first year of life (Piaget, 1954). Evidence for infant use of these cognitive processes in solving problems has been described by Harris (1983). The rate and quality of the competences will be determined initially by the family experience of the child interacting with biogenetic characteristics of the child. The distancing interactions children have with family members and subsequent socializing agents, such as teachers or peers, are varied, and it is these variations in kind that influence the nature of the individual differences in the trajectories of representational competence (Sigel, 1981; Sigel and Cocking, 1977). Scarr-Salapatek (1976, p. 166) summarizes the argument well when she writes, "The species pattern . . . is not an unfolding of some genetic program but a dynamic interplay of genetic preadaptations and developmental adaptations to features of the caretaking environment. Individual variation is limited by canalization, on the one hand and by common human environments (for example, family experience), on the other."

Distancing Strategies as the Central Environmental Influence on the Course of Representational Competence

A body of research can be interpreted in the framework of the distancing model I have presented for the early years of life. It has been demonstrated that the preverbal infant engages in mutually reciprocal relationships that involve infants developing expectations of parents' interactions and parents' violating these expectations thereby creating discrepancies (Kagan, 1984). The reciprocal behavioral interactions vary among parents as a function of personal-social characteristics of the participants and the context defining the quality and quantity of interaction. Brazelton and others (1979, p. 41), working within a cybernetic framework, present data that allow for the conclusions: "Each disruption of the system [interlocking feedback of a mutually regulated system of mother-father-infant] allows for separation, differentiation, and individuation for each member of the triad. With reorganization, the feeling of equilibrium and of resynchronization is achieved by each member." Other investigators also report that parents, varying in the quality, type, and frequency of interaction with their children, provided experiences that in my framework can be considered as distancing behavior (Pedersen and others, 1979). In each of these studies, infants show a primitive sense of anticipation, memory, and symbolic interaction—in effect representational competency. Brazelton and others (1979), however, point out that perturbation occurs (in my terms, extreme discrepancies) when the parents' responses to their children are tightly controlled and inflexible. Consequently, differentiation of self from parents may become pathological. This is another argument for the requirement that unless reciprocal interactions are within the child's developmental level, outcomes can be negative. This conclusion argues for a match between the child's capability to comprehend and the child's ability to engage with parental demands.

A number of studies addressing teaching styles has reported that highly directive and didactive parents who paid relatively little attention to the child's interests and abilities tended to develop children with limited linguistic and cognitive competency. These studies have not sought long-term consequences of such experience (Nelson, 1973; Rubenstein and Howes, 1976). In sum, early experiences provide the initial opportunities for the child to differentiate self from others and to begin to function increasingly as a "thinker." I contend that early prototypes of distancing behaviors contribute significantly to the child's development of representational competence. In this way the groundwork is laid for the development of representations of self and of others (Piaget, 1954).

Let me turn now to a discussion of my research program, which links conceptually with the infant studies, supporting my hypothesis that parental teaching styles that make minimal demands on children's inherent representational abilities hinder their cognitive development. But when parents and other significant socializing agents provide learning environments that "force" the child to function as an autonomous, reflective person, representational competence will be enhanced.

Effects of Parents' and Teachers' Distancing Strategies

Two sets of data will be described, one set from our family research program, and the other from two preschool programs. These data show that to the degree that parents restrict the child's opportunities for active engagement in problem-solving the child's representational competence will be restricted. Causal attributions can only be conceptual, since we do not have longitudinal data. I can only infer that what we observed in the teaching situation and in the child-testing situation is a product of the historical relationship between parents and children's developing competence.

Our research program was theory-driven, with a priori hypotheses derived from the aforementioned distancing theory. The model was replicated with three populations allowing for comparisons of different size and social class as well as families containing language-handicapped children. The basic hypothesis guiding each of our studies holds that parents' use of structuring and low-level distancing strategies would correlate negatively to children's representational competence and vice versa for high-level distancing strategies.

Three hundred and sixty families were involved in three studies, which began in 1976. Two hundred and forty families in the first two studies were Caucasian, representing the working and the middle class, each family with a target child between the ages of three-and-a-half and five-and-a-half years (Sigel, 1982; Sigel and McGillicuddy-DeLisi, 1984; Sigel, McGillicuddy-DeLisi, and Johnson, 1980). The third study involved one hundred and twenty families, half of which had a communication-handicapped child, and the other half of which served as controls. The target children were between the ages of three-and-a-half and five-and-a-half years. The data gathered for all studies were similar, with variations depending on the nature of the children's handicaps.

Each family came into our laboratory and engaged in the following tasks: an interview focusing on parents' behaviors and beliefs about children, a teaching situation in which one parent was instructed to teach two tasks to his or her child, a paper-folding origami task, and a story. These were dyadic situations—the father and his child, and the mother with the same child. Children were then taken to a separate room and administered a battery of tasks assessing various aspects of anticipation and memory. The parent-child teaching situations were all videotaped and coded on the structure and level of distancing strategy.

Relationship Between Parent Distancing and Child's Performance on Standardized Tests of Mental Ability. Relationships between parents' use of distancing and children's cognitive abilities as assessed by standard measures of intellectual development generally supported the notion that the type of distancing strategies used by parents affects intellectual development (see Table 2).

The pattern of results shows that correlations for standard intelligence performance and use of low-level demands by parents is related to lower performance scores of children. There were relatively few indications, however, that parents' use of high-level distancing strategies was associated positively with their children's performance on standardized tests.

The finding that relationships were stronger for communication-handicapped (CH) children than for noncommunication-handicapped children (NCH) leads us to consider the very real possibility that the parent was not stimulating the growth of ability in the child as much as she or he was reacting to the existing ability level, or at least her or his perception of the child's ability. That is, the association between low-level distancing by parents and children's intellectual performance may be due to the fact that parents correctly perceive their child's ability level, and when it is low, their conversations with children contain more low-level demands as they attempt to "match" quality of stimulation to the child's capabilities. I will return to this possibility in a later discussion. At this point, it is necessary to investigate relationships between parental distancing and children's performance on tasks designed specifically to assess representational thinking.

Relationship Between Parents' Distancing and Children's Representational Abilities. Relationships between parents' use of distancing and children's performance on the conservation, anticipatory imagery, repro-

Table 2. Correlations Between Frequencies of Parental Distancing Strategies and Children's Scores on Tests of Intelligence

		Group and Test									
		CH Children					Non-CH Children				
Story task behaviors[a]		Verbal WPPSI	Performance WPPSI	PPVT Raw	Raven's Total	Crichton Total	Verbal WPPSI	Performance WPPSI	PPVT Raw	Raven's Total	Crichton Total
High Level	M	.29*	.28*	-.05	-.08	-.02	-.07	.07	.01	-.09	.05
	F	.35*	.36*	.06	.08	.09	-.01	.00	-.17	-.02	-.09
Low Level	M	-.51*	-.52*	-.53*	-.53*	-.46*	-.24	-.16	.21	-.25*	-.01
	F	-.48*	-.43*	-.64*	-.54*	-.48*	-.33*	-.24	-.29*	-.09	-.29*
Questions	M	.08	.11	-.40*	-.42*	-.39*	-.19	-.15	.06	-.16	.05
	F	-.13	-.10	-.28*	-.36*	-.33*	-.07	-.09	-.26*	.03	-.24
Statements	M	-.12	-.17	-.23	-.34*	-.20	-.10	-.09	.05	-.15	-.11
	F	.04	-.00	-.47*	-.27*	-.22	-.17	-.17	-.24	-.14	-.22
Paper task behaviors											
High Level	M	.26*	.24	.13	.03	-.00	-.04	.01	.08	-.04	-.01
	F	.23	.16	-.05	-.02	-.15	-.02	-.00	-.03	.30*	.10
Low Level	M	-.36*	-.38*	-.19	-.29*	-.19	-.09	-.18	-.05	-.05	-.08
	F	-.25*	-.24	-.15	-.13	-.13	-.10	-.13	.05	-.11	.03
Questions	M	.17	.14	-.08	-.11	-.22	.04	.01	.02	-.10	-.06
	F	.10	.11	-.18	-.18	-.35*	-.04	-.10	-.25*	-.01	-.14
Statements	M	-.06	-.16	.10	-.16	.03	-.07	-.26*	-.01	-.11	-.05
	F	.30*	.25*	.08	.22	.25*	-.14	-.18	.20	.09	.15

[a] M = Mothers; F = Fathers   * p < .05

58

ductive memory, and object classification tasks used have been reported elsewhere (Sigel, 1982). To briefly summarize the findings, mothers' use of high-level distancing was related to children's anticipatory imagery and object classification performance, whereas fathers' distancing strategies were related to children's memory performance. These relationships were significant even after social class and family-constellation factors were taken into account.

Correlations between frequencies of parent distancing strategies and children's performance on representational tasks are reported separately for CH and NCH children in Table 3. With respect to NCH children's performance, mothers' and fathers' levels of distancing during the paper task were related to anticipatory imagery in directions proposed by the distancing theory. In addition, mothers who used statements frequently had children who were less successful on this task. Low-level distancing by both parents during the story-telling task was negatively related to NCH children's performance on the memory and sequencing task and memory for sentences task. As Table 3 indicates, children whose parents frequently used low distancing demands tended to score lower on most of the representational ability tasks.

A similar pattern was observed in the sample of CH children, although the magnitude of the relationships is slightly higher for the CH children than for the NCH children. In addition, both fathers' and mothers' use of high-level distancing behaviors during the story interaction was associated with higher levels of performance of CH children on anticipatory imagery and seriation problems. The children of mothers who used high-level distancing strategies during the paper-folding task achieved higher anticipatory imagery and memory for sentences scores.

The relationships between verbal teaching strategies that vary along a distancing dimension and children's performance on these tasks provide support for our hypothesis that higher-level distancing strategies stimulate children to engage in representational thinking. These findings suggest that parents match the level of their cognitive demands to the capabilities of the child, but the findings also support the idea that the parents' use of higher levels of distancing relate to the children's ability to demonstrate high anticipatory and memory skills. Parents' behaviors have an impact in promoting such skills. It is worth noting the association between high-level demands of parents and high levels of representational ability in the child and the association between low-level demands of parents and lower performance levels on such tasks by children. We suspect that, in fact, the direction of influence is mutual, with parent affecting child and child affecting parent. It was found that parents of bright children tended to use high-level strategies and parents of less bright children use low-level strategies. Parents do not operate in isolation of feedback from the child; and a match has occurred, for whatever reason, with increased demands for rep-

Table 3. Correlations Between Frequencies of Parental Distancing Strategies and Children's Scores on Representational Task

Story task behaviors[a]	Group and Task											
	CH Children						Non-CH Children					
	Antici-pation	Memory Sequencing (Familiar)	Memory Sequencing (Geometric)	Seria-tion	Memory for Sentences	Simon	Antici-pation	Memory Sequencing (Familiar)	Memory Sequencing (Geometric)	Seria-tion	Memory for Sentences	Simon
High Level												
M	.30*	-.01	-.01	.26*	.11	.12	.06	.08	.06	-.06	-.01	-.19
F	.37*	.19	.03	.39*	.16	.24	.10	.13	.18	-.04	.05	-.03
Low Level												
M	-.51*	-.54*	-.44*	-.44*	-.43*	-.41*	.11	-.36*	-.30*	-.27*	-.43*	-.22
F	-.34*	-.40*	-.29*	-.20	-.39*	-.41*	-.02	-.39*	-.24	-.21	-.30*	-.23
Questions												
M	.15	-.04	-.04	.02	-.01	.04	.03	-.13	-.16	-.23	-.10	-.25*
F	.04	-.03	-.11	.11	-.11	-.09	.07	-.06	.05	-.16	-.17	-.13
Statements												
M	-.27*	-.35*	-.24	-.12	-.23	-.18	.08	-.21	-.11	-.10	-.38*	-.10
F	-.11	-.21	-.14	.07	-.08	-.09	.06	-.28*	-.24	-.08	-.09	-.14
Paper Task Behaviors												
High Level												
M	.30*	.01	.01	.24	.27*	.18	.01	.08	-.05	-.20	-.08	-.11
F	.17	.08	.05	.15	.00	.11	.32*	.18	.18	.18	-.01	-.21
Low Level												
M	-.31*	-.35*	-.30*	-.34*	-.34*	-.35*	-.27*	-.08	-.16	-.24	-.15	-.21
F	-.09	-.25*	-.20	-.01	-.30*	-.27*	-.05	-.12	-.07	.04	.04	-.30*
Questions												
M	.20	-.05	-.07	.03	.12	-.03	.16	-.10	-.12	-.20	-.10	-.18
F	.16	.00	-.02	.08	-.13	.06	.26*	-.07	-.08	.03	-.12	-.28*
Statements												
M	-.08	-.24	-.21	.01	-.02	-.02	-.39*	-.20	-.15	-.14	-.30*	-.17
F	.22	.10	.10	.24	.15	.11	.03	-.11	-.00	.14	-.08	-.12

[a] M = Mothers; F = Fathers   * p < .05

resentation when the child is at higher developmental levels and thereby likely to benefit from such challenges (Sigel and McGillicuddy-DeLisi, 1984; Sigel, McGillicuddy-DeLisi, Flaugher, and Rock, 1983).

With respect to the particular challenges of the CH child, parents seem quite capable of adopting strategies to meet the challenge. The parents continue to use verbalizations that contain high-level demands, although they simultaneously use more low-level strategies than parents of non-CH children. The strength and direction of the relationships between high- and low-level distancing by parents and children's performance on the representational tasks suggest, at the least, that the distancing content of parents' verbalizations is an important factor in the CH child's development.

Since the research studies were limited to a narrow age range and were not developmental in design, the question is still open as to whether parent-child distancing interactions do set the stage for subsequent cognitive functioning. At this stage of the research effort, I have no direct evidence as to whether this is the case. The conceptualization of this research argues that the distancing strategies do chart the course for future development because parents are probably consistent in their distancing approaches and do not change their basic approaches. This consistency will reinforce the development of the particular representational competence of the child. Current research efforts are underway to examine these very issues.

Evidence from Other Sources Supporting the Distancing Model. Two sets of research with parents report consistent findings regarding the effect of parental direct control strategies in teaching and in discipline. Hess and McDevitt (1984) found that mothers' intervention techniques used at age four relate to school-related abilities at ages five to six and twelve. They write: "Intervention techniques that maximize parental dominance (direct control tactics) were distinguished from those that deemphasize dominance and rely on the child's capacity for self-regulation (indirect control techniques). . . . In both teaching and disciplinary situations, direct control tactics were negatively correlated with children's school-relevant performance (Hess and McDevitt, 1984, p. 2017).

Hess and McDevitt's statement can be interpreted as evidence for the negative impact of direct control strategies (low-level distancing) on school-relevant performance. The answer to this question, at the moment, is conceptual. The other report is from Japan, where it was found that maternal teaching and communication strategies identified at three-and-a-half and four years of age related to IQ performance at ages six and eleven and school performance at age twelve (Kashiwagi and others, 1982). In each case, early direct control strategies related negatively to later IQ and school achievement, while active engagement through conversation related positively.

I interpret these studies as supporting my contention that support for the child's active outreach engaging the environment encourages autonomous problem solving. I should clarify that these active engagements through dialogue and inquiry are but one class of teaching and management that provide opportunities for children to acquire and to utilize their accumulated knowledge in a flexible, productive way. Direct control strategies minimize such opportunities for exploration and seeking and trying alternatives.

A final word about the role of inquiry in view of my previous stress on inquiry as a teaching strategy—it is important to clarify an important revision we had to make in categorizing our data. A heavy reliance on the *form* of the communication as the most significant factor may tend to minimize the role of the content. The high-level distancing demands, while initially planned to be classified on the basis of form as well as content, eventually were separated on the basis of content level, that is, the cognitive message to the child (see Table 1). The message indicates demands for action, and as the results indicate, cognitive outcomes seem to be based on the content more than on the form of the communication from the parent (Pellegrini and Greene, 1980).

A related concern has to do with the sequence in which inquiry was used by parents. Preliminary findings reveal that the use of high-level distancing strategies in dialogic patterns relate positively to children's mnemonic competence (Zahaykevich and others, 1985). Follow-up questions in preschool also have a positive effect on children's performance on problem-solving tasks (Rosner, 1978).

Each of these studies corroborates previous research by others demonstrating that highly controlled, didactic communication tends to relate negatively to mental competence, while communications that foster active participation show positive outcomes. I do not have assessments of parent-child interactions prior to the preschool period, so I do not know whether the parents in my studies use comparable communication strategies from infancy periods. Presumably, the evidence that the family environment does play a role in influencing children's representational competence is suggested not only by my work but also by the work of others (Bretherton and Waters, 1985). Furthermore, I can identify the types of parental teaching styles that do have a positive as well as a negative influence on children's representational competence. To the best of my knowledge, the negative results should be interpreted as a relative depression in competence. There was no evidence of developing mental retardation. I interpret these results to mean that children's representational competence will be depressed to the degree that they grow up in homes in which the cognitive demands are not high level and in which parents tend to disregard children's interests and exploratory needs.

Evidence from Preschool. Two preschool studies were done using the same distancing strategy model. One used a group of two-and-a-half-year-old black children from poverty-stricken homes. They were enrolled in a four-and-a-half-day-per-week program. Teachers were trained and supervised by me in the use of distancing strategies. The materials that were developed were calibrated to accent the children's developmental level (Sigel, Secrist, and Forman, 1973). The children remained in the program until they were five. Employing a battery of tests evaluating the basic representational competency, we found that although the children had had a slow start, when they were five years old, they were capable of engaging in every task in the battery appropriate for their age.

A follow-up study done by Cataldo (1978) revealed that children from our early childhood education (ECE) program were in the upper quartile of their second-grade elementary school class in reading and mathematics, performing significantly better than children who had had no preschool experience or who had merely had custodial day care. Since the ECE program was built on the distancing model and was carefully monitored, it is safe to assume the outcome of the ECE program can be attributed in part to the distancing model.

A second nursery school project was established at the Educational Testing Service with children from middle-income families on the assumption that middle-class families would vary in their distancing strategies (an assumption verified by our later family studies). The children in this study were four years old and stayed in the program for only one year before entering kindergarten elsewhere. Basically, the format and program were similar to those employed in the previous preschool study, with appropriate adaptations for age and background of the children. The results of this program revealed that children in the distancing strategy program outperformed children in a less cognitively oriented program for language usage and comprehension, memory, and prediction tasks (Cocking, 1979).

Summary and Conclusions

The distancing strategy model was developed as an approach to studying the social genesis of representational competence in children. "Distancing" was proposed as a label describing teaching strategies, irrespective of source, that make cognitive demands on the person and in so doing serve to separate him or her mentally from the ongoing present. Three levels of distancing strategies were identified (see Table 1). Hypotheses were listed to assess the relationship between distancing strategies and representational competence in two preschool programs and with 320 families with preschoolers. The results are consistent—the use of lower-level strategies (minimal cognitive demands such as to label, to describe) relate negatively to representational competence. Preschool experience wherein teachers were trained to use higher-level strategies yielded positive results.

Reconceptualizing studies by others revealed that low-level maternal preschool strategies influence children's IQ and school performance at six and eleven years of age, respectively. That parental teaching strategies show such long-term effects is strongly suggestive that patterns laid down during the formative years have a continuing influence. Whether what was observed in the families we studied when children were preschoolers was an extension of earlier experience is speculative. It seems reasonable to believe that parents' interactions with their children at ages three-and-a-half to five years do not spring de novo, but rather, reflect historical familial patterns. Arguing that there is some continuity in parents' basic orientation to their children, my data strongly suggest that the kinds of cognitive demands parents make on their children reflect basic dispositions that were probably present from much earlier times. Further research will be needed to test this idea.

The findings of these studies implicate the social interactions, especially distancing behaviors, as an ongoing influence on children's developing representational competence. Integrating the social variables of the type described in this chapter will contribute to the development of a more comprehensive theory addressing the significance of early experience for later cognitive functioning. The incorporation of these social variables sets the stage for children's entry into the social environment. Which environmental opportunities are grasped and how they are used depends in part on the patterns laid down by early home experiences (Gottfried, 1984).

References

Brazelton, T. B., Yogman, M. W., Als, H., and Tronick, E. "The Infant as a Focus for Family Reciprocity." In M. Lewis and L. A. Rosenblum (Eds.), *The Child and Its Family*. New York: Plenum, 1979.

Bretherton, I., and Waters, E. "Growing Points of Attachment Theory and Research." *Monographs of the Society for Research in Child Development*, 1985, *50* (entire serial no. 209).

Bullock, M. "Causal Reasoning and Developmental Change over the Preschool Years." *Human Development*, 1985, *28*, 169–191.

Cataldo, C. Z. "A Follow-Up Study of Early Intervention." *Dissertation Abstracts International*, 1978, *39*, 657A. (University Microfilms No. 7813990)

Cocking, R. R. "Preschool Education and Representational Thinking: The Impact of Teacher 'Distancing' Behaviors on Language and Cognition." Unpublished manuscript, Educational Testing Service, Princeton, N.J., 1979.

Gottfried, A. W. (Ed.). *Home Environment and Early Cognitive Development: Longitudinal Research*. New York: Academic Press: 1984.

Harris, P. L. "Infant Cognition." In P. H. Mussen (Ed.), *Handbook of Child Psychology* (4th ed.) Vol. 2. New York: Wiley, 1983.

Hess, R. D., and McDevitt, T. M. "Some Cognitive Consequences of Maternal Intervention Techniques: A Longitudinal Study." *Child Development*, 1984, *55*, 2017–2030.

Hunt, J. M. *Intelligence and Experience*. New York: Ronald Press, 1961.

64

Kagan, J. *The Nature of the Child.* New York: Basic Books, 1984.

Kashiwagi, K., Azuma, H., and Miyake, K. "Early Maternal Influences upon Later Cognitive Development Among Japanese Children: A Follow-Up Study." *Japanese Psychological Research,* 1982, *24,* 90–100.

Kelly, G. A. *The Psychology of Personal Constructs.* Vols. 1 and 2. New York: Norton, 1955.

McCall, R. B. "The Development of Intellectual Functioning in Infancy and the Prediction of Later IQ." In J. D. Osofsky (Ed.), *The Handbook of Infant Development.* New York: Wiley, 1979.

Nelson, K. "Structures and Strategies in Learning to Talk." *Monographs of the Society for Research in Child Development,* 1973, *38,* (serial no. 149), 1–2.

Pedersen, F. A., Yarrow, L. J., Anderson, B. J., and Cain, R. L., Jr. "Conceptualization of Father Influences in the Infancy Period." In M. Lewis and L. A. Rosenblum (Eds.), *The Child and Its Family.* New York: Plenum, 1979.

Pellegrini, A. D., and Greene, R. "The Use of a Sequenced Questioning Paradigm to Facilitate Associative Fluency in Preschoolers." *Journal of Applied Developmental Psychology,* 1980, *1,* 189–200.

Piaget, J. *The Psychology of Intelligence.* (M. Piercy, Trans.) London: Routledge and Kegan Paul, 1950.

Piaget, J. *The Construction of Reality in the Child.* (M. Cook, Trans.) New York: Basic Books, 1954.

Piaget, J. *Success and Understanding.* (A. J. Pomerans, Trans.) Cambridge, Mass.: Harvard University Press, 1978.

Plomin, R., and DeFries, J. C. "Genetics and Intelligence: Recent Data." *Intelligence,* 1980, *4,* 15–24.

Polanyi, M. *Personal Knowledge.* Chicago: University of Chicago Press, 1958.

Rosner, F. C. "An Ecological Study of Teacher Distancing Behaviors as a Function of Program, Context, and Time." *Dissertation Abstracts International,* 1978, *39,* 760A. (University Microfilms No. 7812235)

Rubenstein, J., and Howes, C. "The Effects of Peers on Toddler Interaction with Mother and Toys." *Child Development,* 1976, *47,* 597–605.

Scarr, S. "Constructing Psychology: Making Facts and Fables for Our Times." *American Psychologist,* 1985, *40,* 499–512.

Scarr-Salapatek, S. "An Evolutionary Perspective on Infant Intelligence: Species Patterns and Individual Variations." In M. Lewis (Ed.), *Origins of Intelligence: Infancy and Early Childhood.* New York: Plenum, 1976.

Sigel, I. E. "The Distancing Hypothesis: A Causal Hypothesis for the Acquisition of Representational Thought." In M. R. Jones (Ed.), *Miami Symposium on the Prediction of Behavior, 1968: Effect of Early Experiences.* Coral Gables, Fla.: University of Miami Press, 1970.

Sigel, I. E. "The Development of Pictorial Comprehension." In B. S. Randhawa and W. E. Coffman (Eds.), *Visual Learning, Thinking, and Communication.* New York: Academic Press, 1978.

Sigel, I. E. "Social Experience in the Development of Representational Thought: Distancing Theory." In I. E. Sigel, D. Brodzinsky, and R. Golinkoff (Eds.), *New Directions in Piagetian Theory and Practice.* Hillsdale, N.J.: Erlbaum, 1981.

Sigel, I. E. "The Relationship Between Parents' Distancing Strategies and the Child's Cognitive Behavior." In L. M. Laosa and I. E. Sigel (Eds.), *Families as Learning Environments for Children.* New York: Plenum, 1982.

Sigel, I. E. "Cognition-Affect: A Psychological Riddle." In D. Bearison and H. Zimiles (Eds.), *Thinking and Emotions.* Hillsdale, N.J.: Erlbaum, 1985.

Sigel, I. E., and Cocking, R. R. "Cognition and Communication: A Dialectic Paradigm for Development." In M. Lewis and L. A. Rosenblum (Eds.), *Interaction, Conversation, and the Development of Language.* New York: Wiley, 1977.

Sigel, I. E., and McGillicuddy-DeLisi, A. V. "Parents as Teachers of Their Children: A Distancing Behavior Model." In A. D. Pellegrini and T. D. Yawkey (Eds.), *The Development of Oral and Written Language in Social Contexts.* Norwood, N.J.: Ablex, 1984.

Sigel, I. E., McGillicuddy-DeLisi, A. V., Flaugher, J., and Rock, D. A. *Parents as Teachers of Their Own Learning-Disabled Children.* Princeton, N.J.: Educational Testing Service, 1983. ETS RR-83-21.

Sigel, I. E., McGillicuddy-DeLisi, A. V., and Johnson, J. E. *Parental Distancing, Beliefs, and Children's Representational Competence Within the Family Context.* Princeton, N.J.: Educational Testing Service, 1980. ETS RR-80-21.

Sigel, I. E., Secrist, A., and Forman, G. "Psycho-Educational Intervention Beginning at Age Two: Reflections and Outcomes." In J. C. Stanley (Ed.), *Compensatory Education for Children, Ages Two to Eight: Recent Studies of Educational Intervention.* Baltimore, Md.: Johns Hopkins University Press, 1973.

Waddington, C. H. "Paradigm for an Evolutionary Process." In C. H. Waddington (Ed.), *Towards a Theoretic Biology II: Sketches.* Edinburgh: Edinburgh University Press, 1969.

Weiner, N. *Cybernetics: Control and Communication in the Animal and the Machine.* New York: Wiley, 1967.

Werner, H. "The Concept of Development from a Comparative and Organismic Point of View." In S. S. Barten and M. B. Franklin (Eds.), *Developmental Processes: Heinz Werner's Selected Writings.* Vol. 1: *General Theory and Perceptual Experience.* New York: International Universities Press, 1978.

Zahaykevic, M., Sigel, I. E., and Rock, D. A. "A Model of Parental Speech Acts and Child Cognitive Development." Unpublished manuscript, Educational Testing Service, Princeton, N.J., 1985.

Irving E. Sigel is a distinguished research scientist at Educational Testing Service in the Division of Education Policy Research and Services, Princeton, New Jersey. During the past ten years he has engaged in a series of studies focusing on the role of the family in cognitive development of children. The research reported in this chapter is based in part on that research program.

*In seeking early influences on the development of competence,
researchers have typically been limited to one or two
generations. Based on evidence from a case study of early
prodigious achievement, it appears that "transgenerational"
influences over several generations may also be at work.
Such influences are not genetic and may be conscious or
unconscious.*

Transgenerational Influences on the Development of Early Prodigious Behavior: A Case Study Approach

*David Henry Feldman,
Lynn T. Goldsmith*

Although developmental psychology is the most comprehensive of the
branches of psychology, it nonetheless has had some difficulty achieving
the long-term time perspective that one might expect. Studies examining
the impact of parental styles and family characteristics on the growing
child have been common (Clarke-Stewart, 1973; Hess and Shipman, 1965;
Yarrow, 1963), but studies attempting to put the life-span in long-range

Much of this chapter was presented at a conference at the Center for
Advanced Study in the Behavioral Sciences at Stanford University on March 11,
1985. The participants in that conference were very helpful, especially Rochel
Gelman, Fran Horowitz, Marc and Shirley Feldman, and Luca Cavalli-Sforza.
Thanks also to Martha Morelock Brown for her help in the preparation of this
manuscript. The work itself was supported by grants from The Spencer Foundation, the Andrew W. Mellon Foundation, and the Biomedical Faculty Grants program at Tufts University.

W. Fowler (Ed.). *Early Experience and the Development of Competence.*
New Directions for Child Development, no. 32. San Francisco: Jossey-Bass, June 1986.

67

perspective have been few and far between. In this chapter we explore possible influences on the child's early development that originate with parents, grandparents, and even more distant family relations. We explore the possibility that some nongenetic influences are handed down from generation to generation, directly or indirectly, that guide and channel the child-rearing decisions and practices found within a family. These "transgenerational" sources of influence, operating across several generations, may provide deliberately articulated maxims or strategies for child-rearing or may represent unstated, background values that have been unconsciously incorporated into each generation's parenting.

The vehicle for considering transgenerational influences on early child development is a case study of the family of the prominent violinist Yehudi Menuhin. In addition to being the subject of several biographies, Menuhin has also written the story of his own life (Menuhin, 1977; Magidoff, 1955; Rolfe, 1978). Feldman has also begun more traditional empirical studies of possible transgenerational influences in child-rearing with students, using unselected groups of families, but this work is still in its early stages. The case study presented here, taken as a starting point, illustrates quite sharply some of the issues that will have to be considered in determining the nature of transgenerational transmission and the extent of its influence. In the Menuhin family, some of these forces seem to have been quite subtle, a matter of family heritage and tradition, while others were quite direct and conscious. The latter seem to be forces the Menuhin parents were aware of, while others only surfaced through the efforts of family members to uncover historical traditions and practices that were present in preceding generations.

This notion of transgenerational transmission is, we think, a new one. Psychologists now agree that the child's early and even prenatal experiences are crucial for future development (for example, Davidson and Short, 1982; Lenzer and others, 1982; Martin, 1976; Moore, 1982), but few have looked for experiences influencing development that predate the months of gestation. It has become almost commonplace to state that the child's early years are crucial in the formation of personality and the crystallization of talent. For example, Freud noted, "If a man has been his mother's undisputed darling, he retains throughout his life the triumphant feeling, the confidence in success, which not seldom brings success along with it" (Clark, 1980, in Howe, 1982). And Bloom wrote that, by the age of four, more than half of the variance in adult intelligence is predicted by the score on an IQ test (Bloom, 1964). These assertions have been widely interpreted to mean that the trajectory of a child's psychological development is set during the preschool years: the foundations of both intellectual capacity and personality are laid by the age of five or six. Such assertions have led to a great interest and activity in trying to determine just what the optimal conditions are for facilitating development in the young child and how to better provide them. The belief that early experiences are central to the course of later development has led to many studies of factors contributing to a good start, especially for children who may be at risk for poor intellectual development (Hess and Shipman, 1965; White, 1970, 1979; Zigler and Valentine, 1979). Others have concentrated on how to provide enriched early environments to boost the potential of already promising children (see Fowler, 1983).

Previous Research

In the search for important qualities of early experience, researchers have cast a rather wide net. Some have concerned themselves with the nature of attachment during the early months of life (Ainsworth and others, 1978; Bowlby, 1982; Rutter, 1981; Spitz, 1965), others have looked at the amount and variety of visual stimulation available (Bower, 1974; Fantz and others, 1975; White and others, 1964), while still others have concerned themselves with nutrition and other health-related issues (Blouin and others, 1983; Dixon and others, 1982; Goggin and others, 1978; Salzarulo and others, 1982; Zeskind and Ramey, 1978). These studies have dealt more with crucial requisite experiences for normal development than with identifying those experiences that might enhance development, even though both—what is a requisite environment for development and what is optimal—are sometimes not distinguished in the literature. During the 1960s, when there was great concern about children from "disadvantaged" backgrounds, investigators focused their attention on parenting styles (Hess and Shipman, 1965), effects of early education programs such as Head Start (Zigler and Valentine, 1979), and infant stimulation programs (Fowler, 1983). Descriptive inquiries of family characteristics that may influence the realization of potential have also been part of this general research movement—for example, IQ studies (Bloom, 1964; Hanson, 1975; Scarr and Weinberg, 1976, 1978) and investigations of children's birth order (Cicirelli, 1967; Zajonc and Marcus, 1975; Zajonc and others, 1979).

In casting their wide net, however, researchers studying early experience have concentrated almost without exception on influences directly affecting the life cycle of the child. The time frame of this body of research encompasses the early experiences of the children themselves: It includes the years of the joint existence of parents and children. A study might begin with prenatal surveys or observations of parents-to-be, but this is about as far back as the data gathering goes. When researchers follow subjects out of early childhood (in longitudinal studies), the work tends to emphasize how the experiences of the first few years of life influence later development. Rarely does the research conceive of development as a set of reciprocal influences of child and environment. (See Bell, 1968; Bell and Harper, 1977; and Clarke-Stewart, 1973, however, for some hints of more reciprocal models.)

While the body of literature dealing with early experiences has made a substantial contribution to our knowledge about the "reaction range" of early development (Gottesman, 1974), within this research tradition the scope of influences tends to be limited to a set of relatively stable characteristics of the child's early environment that has a bearing on the adequacy of development during the first few years. To oversimplify, it seems as if researchers have been looking at the child's early years for some magic formula for providing the kinds of experiences that will guarantee growth and development. From time to time programs are offered that even claim to provide optimal conditions for development (the one most visible today is the intense method of early stimulation propounded by Doman, intended to bring out the "genius" in every child) (Doman, 1975, 1979). The particular content of such programs of stimulation need not be examined here; it is enough to recognize that they carry the assumption that the infant's or young child's experience before the age of six or so will determine to a significant degree what the outcome of development will be. Not all programs are as extreme in their claims as Doman's Better Baby Institute, but the assumption is similar: do the right things early and you have guaranteed your child the best chance of becoming a genius, or at least of doing as well as possible in the game of life.

To a certain extent it is no doubt true that early experience influences later development. What is difficult to determine is the importance of any particular experience for various kinds of developmental issues. How crucial, for example, is it for a future mathematician to be exposed to numbers and counting during the preschool years? How important is it for the future poet to have language-related experiences as part of the daily routine? What kinds of language exercises or experiences should they be? There are few answers to questions such as these. The discussions of early experiences tend to take place on a much broader level. For example, it might be argued that it is crucial to language development for all children to have an attentive adult speak to them and provide feedback on the development of their speech production (see Holzman, 1983). Yet, from the work of Piaget and others, it seems clear that early development is amazingly robust: At least for the major milestones of cognitive development, it appears that the range of experience sufficient for normal development to proceed is extremely large. Whether or not development proceeds "optimally" is another question, and a very difficult one to answer. To know whether a child is developing to his or her full potential, we would need to be able to assess potential itself, which, of course, we cannot do. At best, we could assume a rough correlation between the richness and variety of early experience and the quality of development. Only at the extremes of deprivation do we have evidence that variations in environmental stimulation make any real difference to the pace of development. Evidence for this has been mounting ever since Gesell and Thompson (1929) tried to accelerate the motor development of one member of a pair of twins only to find that such development seemed to be controlled as much by the maturational timetable as by environmental intercessions, if not as much as Gesell originally claimed (Fowler, 1962; Razel, 1985). Very little research indicates that general developmental progress is much affected by targeted stimulation efforts. But what about acceleration of development within specific fields?

Here there is little research to inform us. Relatively little is known about the relationships between specific early experiences in various domains and the later competence that is developed in these domains, perhaps because researchers had hoped to find general principles of early stimulation that would ensure adequate if not optimal development. An important recent exception is the work of Bloom and associates, who interviewed 120 world-class performers in six different highly demanding fields (Bloom, 1985). Although the data are retrospective (the subjects were generally in their thirties when interviewed), they shed some light on the kinds of experiences that seemed important to these individuals' later achievement. Interestingly, while few subjects reported that specific experiences in their subject matter areas were a major part of their first six years or so, field-related experiences were often an important feature of their early lives. These impressions were confirmed by their parents as well. What did occur with some frequency was that fields were valued, encouraged, and taught to the children by their parents. For example, for the musicians interviewed, it was common for one or both of the subjects' parents to be interested in music or to be accomplished musicians themselves. Music was a natural and active part of daily living from the earliest days in the child's life. Indeed, some families seemed surprised to hear that it was different in anyone else's house! To some extent this tendency to have created, without contrivance, an environment for music (or art or sports or academic pursuits) was a spontaneous and unself-conscious tendency by the parents of these future world-class performers. Yet even these tendencies were not typical of Bloom's families, at least in all fields:

> Indeed, contrary to what we might expect, most of our swimmers did not come from homes in which swimming was presently, or had been, a part of either parent's routine. We estimate that slightly less than 30% of our sample had at least one parent with some background in competitive swimming. The quality and extent of these backgrounds ranged from a season or two at the YMCA to many years of Amateur Athletic Union (AAU) and other pre-Olympic competition. On the other hand, almost 75% of the swimmers had at least one parent with a definite, though usually passive, interest in athletics. . . . these parents saw the value of sports and competition and encouraged their children to get involved in both (Bloom, 1985, p. 145).

Bloom's research suggests that if early experience in a specific field is important, it is apparently not a straightforward relationship. Bloom found wide variation in how systematically children had been exposed to a field, indeed in the extent to which they were exposed at all. In fields where practice does not begin until adulthood (such as neurosurgery), it is difficult to see any specific early events that might have connected to later experience in which the course of a career was shaped. The relationship between specific kinds of early experiences and later capability is thus neither clear nor obvious. At the general level, there are no doubt some constraints on the kinds of conditions that are sufficient to guarantee healthy, normal development, but the latitude seems to be quite large, so large in fact that only in extreme cases of deprivation do there seem to be significant negative effects on general developmental progress.

For more specific fields of expertise, there are some weak relationships between certain kinds of early opportunities in a field and later achievement within that domain. These relationships, however, do not seem to hold for all fields or for all participants in any particular field. A more complex, subtle, and sensitive kind of analysis seems to be called for if we are to establish a relationship between early experience and later development within specific fields. It is in the spirit of this need to consider possibilities that extend beyond those studied thus far that we propose the possibility of transgenerational influences on development. These influences require extending the time frame for affecting development to include influences that may come from pre-parental generations. Parents themselves may be aware of some of these influences and make conscious use of them in their child-rearing; other influences may not even reach their consciousness. We will use the rearing of virtuoso violinist Yehudi Menuhin to show that such influences may be present, at least in extreme cases. And we use this admittedly unusual case to detect some possibilities about how transgenerational influences might occur in less extreme situations.

Transgenerational Influence: Possible Sources

The notion underlying transgenerational influences on development is that historical family traditions, values, myths, and interests, filtered through child-rearing practices, may represent a significant type of early experience for the child. Thus, transgenerational influences would include any and all sources of child-rearing that have their origin in earlier generations of ancestors, as well as influences that are of a physical, behavioral, psychological, or traditional nature.

Two sources of transgenerational influence have appeared in the psychological literature over the years, although not with this label: one relatively widely accepted, one quite peripheral and lacking in acceptance. The first is the genotypic influence of one generation on another through genetic transmission. Physical characteristics and some behavioral traits have been found to run in families, and selective breeding experiments with plants and animals have indicated that certain traits can be enhanced or eliminated. The idea that certain qualities of intellect run in families has also had a fair amount of support since at least Galton's time (Galton, 1891). Therefore, there has been acceptance of the notion that there can be an ancestral influence on the child in the form of a shared (or transmitted) genetic substrate. While transgenerational influences have thus been considered at the level of genetic transmission of traits, it must be noted that these influences do not really consistitute early experiences for the child, but rather they affect his or her predispositions and proclivities toward experiencing and organizing the world.

The second source of transgenerational influences appearing in the literature derives from the Jungian tradition of archetypes. Jung argued that certain universal images and themes run throughout human history, passed along from family member to family member. Images such as the patriarch, the father, the earth, the mother, the Christ, and their attendant myths live in the collective unconscious of humanity, in part as a result of family transmission from generation to generation (Bolen, 1979). The degree to which one or another of these images dominates and influences an individual's experiences is to a great extent a transgenerational matter, as we shall see in the case of the Menuhin family. The precise mode of transmission of Jungian archetypes is unknown (or perhaps the word *communication* is more accurate), but somehow the universal images are passed from generation to generation, and the particular set that is most salient for any individual is largely a matter of which archetypes were most central to his or her ancestors.

Without further comment on these sources of possible transgenerational influence, let us proceed to some other possible sources of influence. Aside from pointing to prior generations as the source of influence on the child's early experience, the concept of transgenerational influence does not yet specify the precise mechanisms of such cross-generational transmission. In fact, the specific mechanisms may well differ with the particular type of influence identified: Genetic transmission quite obviously involves a biological mode, while others most likely involve forms of interpersonal communication—either overt or covert—of values, beliefs, or ways of behaving. Speculation about mechanisms of transfer must await further work.

As an organizational matter, let us divide possible transgenerational influences on development into those that are first observed in the behavior of parents and those that are first observed in their children. The most important parental factor for this discussion is the tendency of certain families to be involved in various fields or professions. Professions often seem to run in families; for example, there are a number of noteworthy musical families (the Bachs are probably the best-known example; also the Mozarts) and artistic families (the Wyeths, the Peales, and the Bruegels). Families tend to maintain certain other traditions perhaps even more often than they preserve occupational roles; for example, religious, class, or caste associations, or family myths (such as whom they are descended from, what role they have played in history, and so on). All of these kinds of influences help to set the large-scale context within which child-rearing takes place. The fact that seven generations of "Smiths" have been teachers or blacksmiths may not have a direct, day-to-day impact on parents' specific child-rearing practices, but this tradition may, in effect, frame the whole child-rearing enterprise as "the preparation of the next generation of Smiths to become teachers or blacksmiths." The religious affiliation of a family may have direct effects on child-rearing. In some instances such influences are profound; for example, in religious groups where all activity is quite closely directed by religious doctrine. Devout Muslim families would no doubt raise their children in dramatically different ways from agnostic families or even from families with only nominal religious affiliations as is common in this country today.

The interesting question, of course, is how influential such macro-level influences are on the identification and development of talent in children. One can imagine, for example, that in a family in which one occupation is quite obviously valued above others, the children with talents for this occupation would be singled out, while children who fail to demonstrate such capabilities may be ignored or discouraged from developing their own talents.

Transgenerational influences associated with the child have to do with the abilities, temperamental qualities, physical characteristics, and interests that begin to appear early in the child's life and that are perceived by parents and other relatives as characteristic of other family members. Whether such qualities are inherited or somehow developed and encouraged through behavioral modeling or some other external process is not clear. What is clear is that parents often begin to connect the behaviors of their children with themselves and those of other relatives: "He takes after Uncle Daniel with a strong will like that." Perhaps a stronger link to family tradition is made: "The Smiths are all strong-willed people." Transgenerational influence may work on quite subtle qualities. For example, some families may recognize and develop a quality like perseverence more actively than others. Social and cognitive flexibility, pragmatism, humaneness, humor, and others may be some of the qualities or characteristics that are subtly shaped by transgenerational values, attitudes, and intentions.

These qualities may represent in part a biological aspect of the family heritage. Nonetheless, tendencies must be met with an organized and comprehending response in order to be durable and significant. The Boston Kennedys have produced three generations of individuals who have become involved in politics and public service. Without this tradition, would the tough, determined, yet public-minded qualities that distinguish this family have gone unexpressed or would they have been expressed differently? Because transgenerational influences involve the combination of family expectations or tendencies with a set of qualities or a pattern of traits within the child, the development of particular quality may proceed only when the joint set of external (family) and internal (child) characteristics and values is present. Indeed, the equation may be still more complex, requiring certain qualities to exist in the broader surroundings, such as sufficient wealth or a particular political system that lends itself to the expression of the capabilities under consideration. Feldman (1980, 1986) has given the label "co-incidence" to the idea that coordination among a number of different forces must take place for the expression of extreme potential. Transgenerational influences represent another one of the co-incidence forces and may contribute to a prediction about competence. When the conditions are right and the forces coincide, extreme forms of the expression of potential may occur, for example, yielding a prodigy.

The notion of transgenerational influence as a factor in the child's early experience, particularly in the recognition and development of talent, arose from Feldman's study of six children exhibiting early prodigious achievement (Feldman, 1986). It seemed necessary to consider the possibility of transgenerational influences on the expression of potential for two reasons: Strains of talent or interest in a field could be found in some of the families studied but not in all of them, leading Feldman to wonder whether this might not at times be a significant influence on children's early experiences and development. The second reason was provided by several accounts Feldman read of other families in which something akin to transgenerational influence seemed to prevail. It is to the most revealing of those cases that we now turn, that of the family of violinist Yehudi Menuhin.

The Menuhins: A Family of Transgenerational Influence

Yehudi Menuhin was perhaps the most celebrated child prodigy of this century. He burst on the music scene at age six, and by eleven was known and applauded as the most gifted youngster to have played the violin in many years. His talent was not limited to technical mastery; he possessed an uncanny ability to interpret music, giving a depth of feeling to passages that challenged the most accomplished professional of any age. A constant figure in the press during his early years, Yehudi Menuhin has also been the subject of books and articles (see especially Magidoff, 1955), has written his own autobiography (Menuhin, 1977), and is still seen frequently on the concert stages of the world, although he has by now passed his seventieth birthday.

There are in fact two accounts of Menuhin's rise to world prominence. The first is the official one, the one that was written by Menuhin himself or his authorized biographers. The second account, while similar in terms of many of the particulars, is vastly different from a psychological standpoint. This account is provided by Menuhin's nephew Lionel Menuhin Rolfe, the son of Menuhin's younger sister Yaltah (Rolfe, 1978). The first account fits well within the developmental framework that Westerners are comfortable with, while the second raises questions about the adequacy of that framework for comprehending (let alone explaining) a phenomenon as unbelievable as a prodigy like Yehudi Menuhin. It was largely through reading Rolfe's book about the Menuhin family that the idea of transgenerational influences on child development was formed.

In the official version of the Yehudi Menuhin story, "history" begins more or less with the marriage of Menuhin's parents and continues through his extraordinary development as a violinist. References to the past (that is, the time before Menuhin's birth) yield little richness of detail; they are mostly brief notes about his parents and tales of their meeting and marriage—tales that support the family myth of the immigrant family making good. The Menuhin myth as presented in the official version of Menuhin's life is the same one that is portrayed thousands of times in television programs, films, magazines, and political speeches. It is the myth of the American dream. In bare outline the story is as follows: Jewish immigrants meet and marry in New York at the turn of the century. They soon see that opportunities lie in the West. They pick up their newborn child (Menuhin) and move to San Francisco. There they settle into an idyllic life, two more children come along, and they begin to build for the future. Menuhin is taken at age two to concerts of the San Francisco Orchestra, and he is mesmerized. He asks to play the violin. He shows great talent and works hard, and before long he is playing concerts and receiving the praise and admiration of the world. Menuhin becomes rich and famous, and the rest of the family also prospers. They all live happily ever after in London as world citizens, where Menuhin and his second wife start a school for promising musicians.

There is of course a great deal more to the story than this summary, but the basic outline is more or less accurate. This is how Menuhin's life story is portrayed. Except, that is, for the story as told by his nephew Lionel Menuhin Rolfe. As was true of many alienated souls during the 1960s, Rolfe was moved to learn about his "roots." As part of the family of the great Yehudi Menuhin, there were too many things that just did not make sense to the then thirtyish Rolfe. Why, for example, did his grandfather, Moshe, now treat him with such total disdain after having been a warm and attentive figure when Rolfe was a small child? Why did everyone in the family seem to worship Menuhin? True, he is a great violinist, but their adoration, particularly that of Rolfe's own mother, Yaltah, seemed to go beyond admiration; it was more like reverence. And perhaps most difficult was how to explain the astounding talent of Menuhin, a talent that comes along perhaps once in a century. Why indeed should Menuhin, who shared a blood tie with Rolfe, be world famous and celebrated, while Rolfe wandered the streets of Los Angeles, living what he himself describes as a "sleazy" existence. For Rolfe the search for an explanation of the strange behavior of his family was also a search for his own identity.

What Rolfe was to learn was that his family had been producing prodigies for several centuries as part of a hereditary dynasty of Hasidic rabbis. Although Menuhin's parents were aware of their past, they chose to cut themselves off as much as possible from this tradition, even to the point of becoming anti-Zionist and possibly anti-Semitic. Yet the tradition of prodigies was to exert a profound influence on the Menuhins, even as they tried to put it behind them. Menuhin's ancestors were the founders of the Lubavitcher Hasidic Jewish tradition, one of the most powerful forces in Eastern European Jewish history, and for a time a potent force among non-Jewish constituencies as well. For about six hundred years, a member of the Schneerson family had been leader of the Lubavitcher movement, up to and often including the present Lubavitcher communities in Israel and Brooklyn, New York. Every generation or so a child appeared whose understanding of the Torah (the Jewish Bible) and the Talmud (the Jewish laws of living) was so dramatically beyond that of his peers that he was placed in the line of succession to become the Lubavitcher Rabbi; virtually all of these prodigy children came from the same family line. Yehudi Menuhin was a product of the same family, since both his father and his mother were direct descendents of the dynasty, although his mother denied it. They were, within this context, almost like royalty. Indeed some of their own experiences as children were with relatives who still lived like royalty.

The important point for our purpose is that as children, none of the Menuhin offspring were aware of their past. Their parents, Moshe and Marutha, knew about their heritage but chose to reject it and begin their own dynasty, with Yehudi as the first great prodigy of the new secular religion, music. As we shall see, the transplanted Menuhins went about beginning the new enterprise in a manner that bore striking similarities to how the Lubavitcher tradition was maintained over the centuries. Yet neither Moshe nor Marutha was reared to become a leader. In fact, the tumultuous years in Europe during the last decades of the nineteenth century were to send each of Menuhin's parents away from their homelands and cut them off from sources of knowledge of who they were and what their place in the community might have been. Marutha's family had moved to the south of Russia from Lubavitch before she was born, while Moshe was sent to Palestine as a young child to live with a grandfather who saw no special promise in the youngster.

Transgenerational Influences. Given this brief account of the two stories of Menuhin's origin and development, how, specifically, do possible transgenerational influences play a part in that story? Does it make more sense than the standard biography version of the Menuhin story to add possible transgenerational influences and long-standing family traditions to the mix? And given these, does it make sense to ask which influences were known to the parents and which were not likely to be known?

There are two qualities of the Menuhin situation that seem most in need of explanation, that seem to fit least well into official versions of their story. The first is the seemingly uncanny ability of the child Menuhin to impart deep feeling to his music. The second is the peculiar behavior of his parents toward him, toward other family members, and also toward outsiders. It is proposed here that the long-standing tendencies in the family, transmitted to both parents and reinforced in their marriage, help account for their behavior. Indeed, after knowing them it is difficult to imagine an explanation that does not acknowledge the importance of these influences from the past. Even this lack of acknowledgement on the part of the Menuhins seems to be their attempt to transcend the past even as they were reliving it.

Here is Rolfe's (1978, pp. 24, 162) description of the young Menuhin's talent:

> My uncle's early music was distinguished from that created by other child prodigies from the same ghetto by its profound and mature interpretation: He has something more than just astounding technique. . . . What was different, the very real miracle of Yehudi's playing, as Bruno Walter recalled of Yehudi's April 1929 Berlin debut, was his "spiritual mastery and maturity." It was at that same concert that Albert Einstein went backstage and hugged Yehudi, saying, "Now I know there is a God in heaven."

Clearly, Menuhin was a prodigy among prodigies. There was something about his playing that could not be accounted for in technical terms. To say that he was "great talent," which of course he was, is also an unsatisfying explanation. What is it that made the talent great? Why was it so extremely and uniquely so in this child and not in other children, even in other children from the same family?

What was different about Menuhin, of course, was that he was descended from a centuries-long line of spiritual leaders of an intensely expressive group of Jews called Lubavitcher Hasids. Music was and is a major part of the Hasidic life, a vehicle for coming into ecstatic relation to God. The violin was not part of that tradition; it had been borrowed from the gypsies as part of the secular movement. But one or more of Menuhin's ancestors was responsible for the composition of spiritual songs that are still sung in Hasidic ceremonies and celebrations. Along with the leadership and music, a tradition of prodigies was also part of his heritage. These prodigies, or *illuy*, as they are called in Hebrew, displayed "precocity not only in music but in science and writing, oratory, and especially religion" (Rolfe, 1978. p. 24). Menuhin's parents chose to break with the tradition of religious life as fully as they could, but clearly they were not to do so altogether. They set about finding and preparing a secular prodigy to carry on the Lubavitcher tradition, although they would vehemently deny any connection between Menuhin's gifts and their spiritual, mystical past as leaders of the Lubavitcher clan.

What the Menuhins did was to try to break with the past by coming to the United States, moving again from New York to San Francisco, and cutting themselves off from virtually all contact with relatives, even from Moshe's brother who also lived in San Francisco. They told their children very little about prior generations. In Menuhin's autobiography it is clear that he has some awareness that he is descended from rabbis, but the tone of the writing makes it clear that little is to be made of this:

> My father is descended from Chasidic rabbis, holders of a hereditary office who kept a court of sorts at Lubavitch, near Gomel, a typical small Russian-Jewish community where the rabbi's spiritual standing gave him temporal authority as well, making him doubly the center of an ingrown society, rejected by the larger society it belonged to but finding sustenance in survival so far and in dreams of Jerusalem for the future. The Chasids, whose movement had its origin in the late eighteenth century, were once rebels among the People of the Book, glorifying ecstatic communion more than legal community, prizing mystics above scholars, and rejecting purely cerebral religion in favor of dancing and making music to the greater glory of God. Such a lively approach to piety would have suited my father's temperament admirably, had not Chasidic spontaneity become institutionalized by his day and he in consequence compelled to rebel anew (Menuhin, 1977, p. 5).

The story of his mother's ancestry is less detailed, and it appears to have been deliberately obfuscated by Marutha herself in an effort to devise her own exotic persona. After fairly extensive research, Rolfe has concluded that Marutha, too, had Schneerson ancestors, although this maternal link to the Lubavitcher dynasty is not acknowledged by the elder Menuhins. Marutha claimed to have been descended from the Tartars. Glossing over her Jewish origins (sometimes even claiming that her father was a Christian), Marutha chose the Crimean warrior tradition as her origin. According to her grandson Rolfe, she maintained that she was a "princess" of some Circassian group. And so, in a way, both father and mother believed they were royalty; they set out to establish a new dynasty in the hills of Los Gatos, California, about thirty miles south of San Francisco. They called their family home Rancho Yaltah, combining in that name the great American West and the Crimean port city in which Marutha was born. The Hasidic tradition was one emphasizing the synthesis of opposites; joining heaven and earth, piety and ecstasy. There, on the West Coast, a new synthesis was about to be forged, unbeknownst even to the people who were forging it.

The Menuhin dynasty was to be built on Yehudi Menuhin's shoulders, having proven through his greatness as a prodigy that the Menuhins were in fact special. They had behaved from the beginning like royalty, had taught Menuhin to do so as well, and they simply would not be pushed into doing otherwise, despite initially modest living circumstances and incomes. Moshe and Marutha believed that Menuhin was second to no one. Not even the great Toscanini was excepted. Much later, when Toscanini invited the sixteen-year-old Menuhin to visit him at his country home near the Mediterranean, Marutha "insisted that if the Maestro wanted to see Yehudi, he should come to Yehudi. She reminded Yehudi not to forget his dignity with Toscanini for he, Yehudi, was also a great maestro" (Rolfe, 1978, p. 164).

It must be recognized that Menuhin was the firstborn (and the only son) in the family. This privileged position may have increased the likelihood that he would become the focus of the family's hopes and ambitions. Though also blessed with considerable talent themselves, his sisters seemed to have been relegated to those traditional roles of supporting and facilitating the development of their older brother. It is Rolfe's (pp. 59, 162) contention that his mother, Yaltah, in particular, languished under the Menuhin regime:

> There was never any suggestion in the Menuhin household that Yaltah could play publicly. . . . If she were going to give a concert, that would only be exploiting the name of her brother and sister. She was told, "Make yourself useful.". . . The parents wove a cocoon from which none of the Menuhin children seem to have escaped, even in their rebellions. The musical career of Yaltah, especially, never matched her talents because of the tightness of her parents' weaving.

Yet despite Menuhin's being given extreme preferential treatment, his legendary charisma and attractiveness seem to have extended to his own family; his sisters "worshipped" and "adored" him to such an extent that Rolfe felt driven to dig into the family's history to find out why. He reports that he was puzzled and hurt when his grandfather, Moshe, brutally rejected him as a young adult after having treated him in a loving and attentive manner as a young child. Perhaps the adult Rolfe was rejected because he had failed to display musical gifts, therefore eliminating him as a candidate to carry on the new family tradition. He was simply irrelevant to the higher purposes of Moshe and Marutha. Rolfe notes that his brother, a theoretical physicist, was apparently no better valued or received by their grandparents than he was. It seems that only certain types of excellence were of any value to the elder Menuhins.

Moshe and Marutha's singlemindedness of purpose, their ruthlessness, their extreme behavior toward different family members (Yehudi and his children versus Yaltah and her sons), seem to require an explanation beyond merely temperament, personality, or preferences for one or another family members. The notion of transgenerational influences may be the sort of organizer to help make sense of such otherwise bizarre behavior. The values and expectations of the dynastic Schneersons were those of an intellectual ruling elite: The preservation and perpetuation of future generations of leaders was a central concern, and potential leaders were accorded special rank. Moshe and Marutha were, in essence, born into families where the tradition existed for extraordinary achievement and hereditary leadership. We would like to suggest that Moshe and Marutha's attitude of noblesse oblige would have prevailed even if their children had not proven to be gifted; but imagine what kind of reception their holier than thou attitude would have received in the skeptical world if Yehudi had been only moderately talented.

The fate of the Menuhin dynasty is uncertain. It now seems clear that no prodigy of Menuhin's stature will come from Moshe and Marutha's grandchildren or great-grandchildren. Perhaps the tradition will continue after a generation or two has passed; Rolfe notes that this has been the case with the ancestral Schneersons. Or perhaps the children's marrying outside of a closely knit Jewish circle—one of the byproducts of their becoming global citizens—will lessen the likelihood of a prodigy appearing, at least one who will carry the familiar qualities. Menuhins of this generation have chosen to marry gentiles, and so the line may be broken. Or perhaps a new line, not tied to a religion or a particular field, will be started in this manner.

A Final Note

In the final chapter of his book, Rolfe tries to find his own interpretation of the Menuhin story. It is a painful effort and not always coherent, but there is a theme running thoughout of poignant yearning for some way of continuing the Menuhin-Schneerson tradition. Perhaps it is Rolfe's way of trying to capture his grandfather Moshe's vision of his family destiny:

82

What of the future of the Menuhins? Coming closer to the Menuhin past has helped me to understand the present-day clan, to see them as participants in a historic transformation. The three Menuhin prodigies (Yehudi, Hepzibah, and Yaltah) were a transition generation . . . from the orthodox Hasidic tradition to the modern world of social activism, revolution, and anarchy. The old cultural mechanisms by which young brainy children were brought into the Menuhin clan are now gone—arranged marriages are out of fashion. A new mix of blood, genes, brains, karma—call it what you will—has entered the Menuhin line and the old gene pool out of which came the Schneersohn dynasty is no more. . . . The Menuhins have tried to become as universal as possible, even if ironically they have remained Hasids in many subtle ways. . . . Perhaps, like my dream, the Menuhins will have happened only once. Yet I know that the world's children will live one day in a New Jerusalem, and that they will create the Utopia that makes New Jerusalems possible (Rolfe, 1978, p. 249).

Through his intense efforts to find himself and explain his strange family, Rolfe has connected with the ascendent tradition that has guided his ancestors and is guiding his relatives to this day. While that set of tendencies does not explain everything that he or his fellow Menuhins have done, it seems a necessary component. It is certainly not the whole story, but it is difficult to imagine the story making much sense without knowing about the history of the Menuhins. This is the point I wish to make about transgenerational influence.

Adding such forces as those that apparently have operated for centuries in the Menuhin family enriches and extends our ability to make sense of their behavior. Certainly with respect to the matter of identification, selection, encouragement, and channeling of talent, it is extremely useful to know that the story of Yehudi Menuhin is a story heavily rooted in the past.

In this chapter we have proposed that there are sometimes influences on early development of talent that come from previous generations in the form of traditions, tendencies, and values. These influences may be as subtle as a feeling of being exceptional or as specific as the need to pick up and move to a particular location. The forces may be conscious or unconscious, direct or indirect. They may operate continuously on each generation or, as in the case of the Menuhins, remain dormant until the conditions are right, until a particularly promising child appears. Whatever the source of transmission of these influences, it is unlikely to be solely genetic in any straightforward sense. Rolfe suggested as much when he speculated about how Moshe and Marutha may have transmitted to the young Menuhin the burden as well as the promise of great musical potential: "If it is true, as composer Felix Mendelssohn said, that music is much more precise a language than words, and thus, what music expresses can only be expressed by music, then perhaps music, even more than something genetic, might have been the way genius was passed down to Yehudi (Rolfe, 1978, p. 85)."

If early experience is to be understood, and particularly if early influences on the development of talent are to be understood, then transgenerational influences will have to be taken seriously. The study of musical ability and achievement in extreme cases like Yehudi Menuhin seems to be a promising place to begin.

References

Ainsworth, M., and others. *Patterns of Attachment: A Psychological Study of the Strange Situation.* Hillsdale, N.J.: Erlbaum, 1978.

Bell, R. Q. "A Reinterpretation of the Direction of Effects in Studies of Socialization." *Psychological Review,* 1968, *75,* 81–95.

Bell, R. Q., and Harper, L. V. (Eds.) *Child Effects on Adults.* Hillsdale, N.J.: Erlbaum, 1977.

Bloom, B. S. *Stability and Change in Human Characteristics.* New York: Wiley, 1964.

Bloom, B. S. (Ed.) *Developing Talent in Young People.* New York: Ballantine, 1985.

Blouin, A. G., Blouin, J. H., and Kelly, J. C. "Lead, Trace Mineral Intake, and Behavior of Children." *Topics in Early Childhood Special Education,* 1983, *3,* 63–71.

Bolen, J. S. *The Tao of Psychology: Synchronicity and the Self.* San Francisco: Harper and Row, 1979.

Bower, T. G. R. *Development in Infancy.* San Francisco: Jossey-Bass, 1974.

Bowlby, J. *Attachment and Loss.* (2nd ed.) Vols. 1–3. New York: Basic Books, 1982.

Cicirelli, V. G. "Sibling Constellation, Creativity, IQ, and Academic Achievement." *Child Development,* 1967, *38,* 481–490.

Clarke-Stewart, K. A. "Interactions Between Mothers and Their Young Children: Characteristics and Consequences." *Monographs of the Society for Research in Child Development,* 1973, *38,* (Serial No. 153).

Davidson, D. A., and Short, M. A. "Developmental Effects of Perinatal Heroin and Methadone Addiction." *Physical and Occupational Therapy in Pediatrics,* 1982, *2,* 1–10.

Dixon, S. D., LeVine, R. A., and Brazelton, T. B. "Malnutrition: A Closer Look at the Problem in an East African Village." *Developmental Medicine and Child Neurology,* 1982, *24,* 670–685.

Doman, G. J. *How to Teach Your Baby to Read: The Gentle Revolution.* Garden City, N.Y.: Doubleday, 1975.

Doman, G. J. *Teach Your Baby Math.* New York: Simon & Schuster, 1979.

Fantz, R. L., Fagan, J. F., and Miranda, S. B. "Early Visual Selectivity." In L. B. Cohen and P. H. Salapatek (Eds.), *Infant Perception.* Vol. 1. New York: Academic Press, 1975.

Feldman, D. H. *Beyond Universals in Cognitive Development.* Norwood, N.J.: Ablex, 1980.

Feldman, D. H. *Nature's Gambit: Child Prodigies and the Development of Human Potential.* New York: Basic Books, 1986.

Fowler, W. "Cognitive Learning in Infancy and Early Childhood." *Psychological Bulletin,* 1962, *59,* 116-152.

Fowler, W. *Potentials of Childhood.* Lexington, Mass.: Lexington Books, 1983.

Galton, F. *Hereditary Genius: An Inquiry Into Its Laws and Consequences.* (2nd ed.) New York: D. Appleton, 1891.

Gesell, A., and Thompson, H. "Learning and Growth in Identical Infant Twins: An Experimental Study by the Method of Co-Twin Control." *Genetic Psychology Monographs,* 1929, *6,* 1-124.

Goggin, J. E., and others. "Observations of Postnatal Developmental Activity in Infants with Fetal Malnutrition." *Journal of Genetic Psychology,* 1978, *132,* 247-253.

Gottesman, I. I. "Developmental Genetics and Ontogenetic Psychology: Overdue Detente and Propositions from a Matchmaker." In A. D. Pick (Ed.), *Minnesota Symposia on Child Psychology.* Vol. 8. Minneapolis: University of Minnesota Press, 1974.

Hanson, R. A. "Consistency and Stability of Home Environmental Measures Related to IQ." *Child Development,* 1975, *46,* 470-480.

Hess, R. D., and Shipman, V. C. "Early Experience and the Socialization of Cognitive Modes in Children." *Child Development,* 1965, *36,* 869-886.

Holzman, M. *The Language of Children.* Englewood Cliffs, N.J.: Prentice-Hall, 1983.

Howe, M. J. A. "Biographical Evidence and the Development of Outstanding Individuals." *American Psychologist,* 1982, *37,* 1071-1081.

Lenzer, I. I., Hourihan, C. M., and Ryan, C. L. "Relation Between Behavioral and Physical Abnormalities Associated with Prenatal Exposure to Alcohol: Present Speculations." *Perceptual and Motor Skills,* 1982, *55,* 903-912.

Magidoff, R. *Yehudi Menuhin: The Story of the Man and the Musician.* New York: Doubleday, 1955.

Martin, J. C. "Drugs of Abuse During Pregnancy: Effects upon Offspring Structure and Function." *Signs,* 1976, *2,* 357-368.

Menuhin, Y. *Unfinished Journey.* New York: Knopf, 1977.

Moore, M. R., and others. "A Prospective Study of the Neurological Effects of Lead in Children." *Neurobehavioral Toxicology and Teratology,* 1982, *4,* 731-739.

Razel, M. "A Reanalysis of the Evidence for the Genetic Nature of Early Motor Development." In I. E. Sigel (Ed.), *Advances in Applied Developmental Psychology.* Vol. 1. Norwood, N.J.: Ablex, 1985.

Rolfe, L. *The Menuhins: A Family Odyssey.* San Francisco: Panjandrum/Aris Books, 1978.

Rutter, M. *Maternal Deprivation Reassessed.* (2nd ed.) Harmondsworth, Middlesex, England: Penguin, 1981.

Salzarulo, P., and others. "Developmental Trend of Quiet Sleep Is Altered by Early Human Malnutrition and Recovered by Nutritional Rehabilitation." *Early Human Development,* 1982, *7,* 257-264.

Scarr, S., and Weinberg, R. A. "IQ Test Performance of Black Children Adopted by White Families." *American Psychologist,* 1976, *31,* 726-739.

Scarr, S., and Weinberg, R. A. "The Influence of Family Background on Intellectual Achievement." *American Sociological Review,* 1978, *43,* 674-692.

Spitz, R. A. *The First Year of Life.* New York: International Universities Press, 1965.

White, B. L. *Human Infants: Experience and Psychological Development*. Englewood Cliffs, N.J.: Prentice-Hall, 1970.

White, B. L. *The First Three Years of Life*. Englewood Cliffs, N.J.: Prentice-Hall, 1979.

White, B. L., Castle, P., and Held, R. "Observations of the Development of Visually-Directed Reaching." *Child Development*, 1964, *35*, 349–364.

Yarrow, L. J. "Research in Dimensions of Early Maternal Care." *Merrill-Palmer Quarterly*, 1963, *9*, 101–114.

Zajonc, R. B., and Marcus, G. B. "Birth Order and Intellectual Development." *Psychological Review*, 1975, *82*, 74–88.

Zajonc, R. B., Marcus, H., and Marcus, G. B. "The Birth Order Puzzle." *Journal of Personality and Social Psychology*, 1979, *37*, 1325–1341.

Zeskind, P. S., and Ramey, C. T. "Fetal Malnutrition: An Experimental Study of Its Consequences on Infant Development in Two Caregiving Environments." *Child Development*, 1978, *49*, 1155–1162.

Zigler, E., and Valentine, J. (Eds.) *Project Head Start: A Legacy of the War on Poverty*. New York: Free Press, 1979.

David Henry Feldman is professor and director of graduate studies at the Eliot-Pearson Department of Child Study, Tufts University.

Lynn T. Goldsmith is a research associate with the Career Development Project at Massachusetts Institute of Technology.

*The early lives of great mathematicians were richly stimulated
in symbol modes that generated semiautonomous cognitive
systems capable of acquiring, processing, and originating vast
complexities of abstract mathematical concepts. Rich early
experiences may be a necessary condition for the full
development of competence potentials.*

Early Experiences of Great Men and Women Mathematicians

William Fowler

If early experience serves important functions in mental development, we
should certainly expect to find evidence for it in the lives of the intellectually great. The inheritance of talent is no guarantee that it will be actual-
ized in competent performance. Genetic factors undergo a complicated
and variable course of cumulative interactions with experience that shape
organismic development across a wide range of phenotypic expression.
But do the early years play any special role in the transformation of genetic
potentials into the complex actualities of cognitive competence? Are there
certain cognitive experiences that *must* occur early in life to ensure exceptional competence in adulthood, either because the young organism is
critically receptive to stimulation or because the type and complexity of
foundation established substantially influences and limits the character of
competences that can develop through later experiences?

Early experience has long been considered important for development. The value of a cognitively salutary environment in the home and
school for facilitating cognitive development and school achievement is
by now well established through the body of studies accumulated over
recent decades (for example, Fowler, 1983; Gottfried, 1984; Walberg, 1979).

W. Fowler (Ed.). *Early Experience and the Development of Competence.*
New Directions for Child Development, no. 32. San Francisco: Jossey-Bass, June 1986.

But the effect of variations in developmental timing is seldom a clear focus. The extended body of early intervention research of recent decades generally supports the concept, but most studies have focused on special, disadvantaged populations whose later adverse experiences appear to have seriously undermined the early cognitive gains derived from special stimulation (Fowler, 1983; Lazar and Darlington, 1982).

Few studies have focused on the role of early experience in the development of intellectual greatness. Yet the importance of specialized early experience is a recurrent theme in the studies and anecdotal case reports of the gifted and talented, notwithstanding historical stress on the biological basis of exceptional ability (Fowler, 1962, 1981, 1983). Despite his genetic bias, Terman's *Genetic Studies of Genius* (1925) and high-ability case studies (1919), for example, are replete with indications of exceptional early experiences. As many as 92 percent of the 246 high IQ, ($\geq$140) "genius" children, where age was indicated, learned to read before age six. Root (1921), more attentive to socialization, rated 87 percent of his 23 high-IQ children superior on early home education. Fowler's (1981) reanalysis of Terman's (1919) 23 high-IQ cases found clear evidence of exceptional early cognitive stimulation in every case.

Investigations of historically eminent achievers have been marked by even less attention to the role of socialization and early experience. Yet, even so great a hereditarian as Galton (1907) concluded, "It is, I believe, owing to the favourable conditions of their early training, that an unusually large proportion of the sons of the most gifted men of science become distingushed in the same career" (pp. 189–190). Cox (1926), too, in her classic study of some three hundred eminent achievers from many fields, though focusing on IQ ratings and performing little systematic analysis of socialization, concluded: "Youths who achieve eminence have, in general, (a) a heredity above the average and (b) *superior advantages in early environment*" (p. 215, emphasis added).

The historical tendency to treat intelligence as a biologically predetermined, global phenomenon (Hunt, 1961) has made it difficult to account for how abilities develop in such varied literary, musical, artistic, physical, scientific, and mathematic forms. Downplaying the role of experience and especially slighting the content particulars of experience, early or otherwise, has delayed understanding of just how experience mediates cognitive development, especially in the development of outstanding competence.

Recently, investigators have become interested in how individuals vary in their abilities among domains and how variations in types of experience, usually beginning quite early, may contribute to these variations (Feldman, 1980; Fowler, 1971, 1977, 1980; Gardner, 1983). Several biographical studies by my students have indicated that the early lives of small (largely) randomly selected samples of leading scientists (Tetroe, 1979), Victorian novelists (Este, 1979), playwrights (Durbach, 1979), and visual artists and architects (Bennett, 1967) have typically been exceptionally stimulating. Bloom and his associates (1985) have recently completed a large-scale retrospective study of the developmental histories of some twenty world-class achievers (aged around thirty-five) in each of a variety of fields, including mathematics, music, sculpture, neurology, and two sports, swimming and tennis. A highly stimulating early life was again a constant, but the domain focus of the special early stimulation in both the Bloom and the student studies was generally—but not always—sharper in certain fields (music and swimming) than in others (visual arts, science, and math).

A study of the developmental histories of the historically exceptionally competent through biography, while presenting problems of control and completeness and accuracy of information, furnishes an unparalleled basis to explore important questions on the relevance of early experience to competence development at the highest levels. The present study was aimed at determining whether special early cognitive stimulation is a necessary though not sufficient factor (a prerequisite) for the development of exceptional competence. The study was designed to investigate the role of early experience more systematically than Cox (1926) and others have, giving special attention to whether early domain focus is a necessary condition for the development of exceptional competence in mathematics, a question that Bloom's studies leave unanswered.

Special early cognitive stimulation has been defined as intensive (frequent) stimulation of complex concepts and abstract symbols, mediated by others (through either formal instruction or informal interaction), and continuing for at least a year before age six. As in the case of great writers and scientists (Fowler, 1983), it was expected that extensive language experiences, early reading, and exposure to complex literary and academic material, well in advance of developmental norms, would be common, but that stimulation in math itself might be less common. The assumption was that verbal symbols and concepts are sufficiently abstract and complex, if stimulated extensively, to pose little difficulty for later transfer to the abstractness and complexity of reasoning with mathematics symbols, as Aiken (1971) and Fowler and Swenson (1979) have suggested. As a corollary, it was expected that the experience of special stimulation early in life would generate exceptional cognitive autonomy in the pursuit of intellectual projects and self-directed study during later development. At issue was whether special early stimulation establishes a cognitive-motivational foundation (critical mass) of a kind capable of generating proportionally greater mental activity and further development autonomously.

A variety of secondary factors were also anticipated to appear in different combinations in different cases. Among these were frequent exposure to a rich intellectual milieu (literary, scientific, academic), informal methods of early stimulation, high family achievement aspirations, intellectual models and mentors, opportunities for special schooling, adequate socioeconomic support throughout childhood, and opportunities for independent play, study, and reflection. These factors were viewed as facilitating development in various ways and combinations, but none of them singly serving as indispensable prerequisites to the development of high competence.

Method

A total sample of twenty-five historically recognized great mathematicians was drawn systematically from two sources. Seven were selected from Osen's (1974) *Women in Mathematics* and eighteen from Bell's (1965) definitive historical anthology, *Men of Mathematics*. The seven women were the entire set of great women mathematicians on whom Osen furnished complete biographical information, after eliminating one woman (Herschel) because her mathematical contributions were so closely linked to those of her elder brother. All cases from the first twenty chapters of Bell were selected, excluding the Greek mathematicians and the many mathematical members of the Bernoulli family because of the dearth of information on their early life histories. Biographical material was collected largely through an exhaustive search of the Harvard University library collections. A mean of 5.3 references was located for each man and 3.4 for each woman. French and Russian sources were translated by me, Italian by Neva Fowler, and German by local translators. The total sample embraces many of the greatest men mathematicians from ancient times to the early nineteenth century and women for all times, excluding non-European sources.

Following my presentation of capsule biographies of early histories and milieux, data on crucial features of early lives are tabulated and discussed in detail. Positive evidence on prerequisite factors emerges with varying degrees of explicitness. Descriptive statements of facts, forms, and ages of early stimulation are of course the most explicit. Descriptions linked in time to other age- or date-recorded events (deaths, remarriages) permit direct inferences on age, however. Less certain but plausible (indirect) inferences on age arise from linkages with lifelong family practices, the presence of an obvious potential mentor, indications of early precocity, indicated but undescribed family educational efforts, and pre-nineteenth-century historical practices of beginning around age three, when home education was undertaken (Daston, 1973; Earle, 1974)—usually seen in various combinations. Negative evidence includes descriptions of unstimulating family practices, low-level cognitive environments, or signs of less than precocious mental development. Lack of evidence is considered to weaken likelihood, rather than to invalidate hypotheses.

Results

Special Early Stimulation. It is immediately evident from the biographical notes and data in Tables 1 and 2 that the early lives of most of these mathematicians were marked by unusual early intellectual experiences. Evidence of special early stimulation ($\leq$ age 5) appears in 15 of the 18 men and 6 of the 7 women (21 cases). Evidence on starting ages was explicit or directly inferrable for 9 of these 15 men and for 4 of the 6 women (13 cases). Age could be indirectly or plausibly inferred for the other 6 of the 15 men and 2 of the 6 women (8 cases). Thus, in only 4 of the total of 25 cases was there little or no evidence of special early stimulation.

Among the thirteen cases with direct evidence, the age of beginning instruction was not always directly recorded but could easily be inferred from the age dating of parallel events. Thus, as seen in Table 1, Abel's father began regularly instructing his son when Abel was three. Descartes's father began his intensive intellectual question-answering immediately following the mother's death, when Descartes was only fourteen months, bringing in formal instruction soon after. Since Leibniz was just six when his father died, the father's extended program of teaching him reading and history must have started several years before, during early childhood. Similarly, for Somerville to read highly advanced material (for example, *Pilgrim's Progress*) by age eight, her mother must have begun to teach her to read some years earlier, during early childhood. Her intellectual interest in nature, stimulated by her father, appeared to date from her earliest years as well.

Among the remaining six men and two women (eight cases) where less direct evidence is available, various indirect indicators of early special stimulation are evident; indicators such as descriptions of family patterns, broad age and precocity descriptors (for example, "very early," "early"), historical context, and similar indicators noted earlier. Such indications are especially prominent in the cases of Euler, Jacobi, Galois, and Breteuil, as Table 1 shows. Precocity is evident in all eight of these cases, moreover, and certain other special signs appear in the other four, which indicate that precocity was rooted in unusually stimulating early intellectual experiences: a boy who "does nothing but study from childhood" (Lagrange); a precocious boy who enters a Benedictine school at age six to become a priest, like his priest (mathematician) uncle who teaches there (Laplace); a destitute architect-surveyor's family that makes special efforts to move to the city to enroll their bright sons in high school (gymnasium) as early as ages seven, eight (Lobatchevsky), and nine; and a bright girl whose home is constantly visited by a stimulating circle of scholars and graduate students around her mathematics professor father (he was physically handicapped) who "strongly influences the early thinking of his children," three of whom become scientists (two mathematicians) and one of whose childhood playmates also becomes a mathematician (Noether).

But what can we say of the three men and one woman for whom there is almost no information on their early childhood experience? Even here there are positive indicators and little to suggest that these mathematicians were not reared from the beginning in less than highly stimulating

Table 1. Milieu and Early Experiences of Great Men and Women Mathematicians

Mathematician	Milieu	Special Early Experiences
Men		
Descartes (1596–1650)	Father: judge, education-oriented. Mother: daughter of a general. Third of four living siblings.	Poor health from birth brought devoted attention from nurse and grandmother. Father stimulated much from fourteen months at mother's death, informally through philosophic-scientific question-answering, gradually shifting to systematic age-graded education, until sent to school at eight.
Fermat (1601–1655)	Father: merchant and consul. Mother came from a family of judges. Uncle-godfather: also a merchant. One brother, two sisters.	Almost nothing known of early life.
Pascal (1623–1662)	Father: judge, specialist in math and old languages. Mother came from a merchant family. One older and one younger sister.	Father gave all schooling (with siblings) from age three (at mother's death); comprehensive; informal methods. Though first down-played, math built into father's concepts. Sickly infancy, but talked early.
Newton (1642–1727)	Mother came from an educated family (Newton's grandmother, uncle); intelligent. Father: uneducated; died before Newton's birth. Stepfather: clergyman. Only child.	Mother was devoted to educating Newton until he was at least three, then she remarried and Newton moved nearby to grandmother; close to mother. Early highly curious, inventive; played mostly alone, but also with girls. Sparse records.
Leibniz (1646–1716)	Father: philosophy professor. Mother was well educated. Studious, scientific home. Older half-brother.	Father taught Leibniz to read, recite passages, and to learn and love history, until he died when Leibniz was six. Mother continued education.
Euler (1707–1783)	Father: pastor; math student of J. Bernoulli. Mother came from a scholarly family. Only child.	Father educated him "very early" (Spiess, 1929, p. 33), teaching and inspiring math "as soon as he could understand" (Pasquier, 1927, p. 2), "with his first notions of ethics and literature" (Fuss, 1839, p. vii). "Gifted boy" with exceptional memory.
Lagrange (1736–1813)	Father: artillery treasurer; speculated. Mother: physician's daughter. First of eleven siblings (two lived).	"He did nothing but study from childhood" (Virey and Potel, 1813, p. 4). Very precocious. Sparse records.

	Family	Education
Monge (1746–1818)	Father and uncle: shopkeepers. Father revered education; wrote well. First of three sons; older sister.	"Father . . . did everything to give his children a solid upbringing and superior education." (Dupin, 1819, p. 4). All brothers became mathematicians. High abilities led to acceptance in special school free at five. Manual experience.
Laplace (1749–1827)	Father: cider producer. Uncle: priest and mathematics teacher at Laplace's first school.	Entered school at six to be in the church. Early precocity and exceptional memory. Sparse records.
Fourier (1768–1830)	Father: master tailor. Ninth of twelve siblings by second wife.	Attended small prep school (age ?). High abilities won patrons to enter Royal Military School at twelve.
Gauss (1777–1855)	Father: accountant, fine calculator and good writer. Mother: stonemason's daughter could read but not write. Uncle: self-educated philosopher.	Early stimulated to calculate (by three) and read (before school) through informal family interaction (calendar numbers, letter sounds); much intellectual discussion with uncle.
Poncelet (1788–1867)	Illegitimate child of rich lawyer-landowner. Adopted by "excellent" family (infancy to fifteen).	Adoptive family saw to his earliest education. Advanced over primary schoolmates; precocious in math and mechanical skills and read many great French plays on own from at least age ten on.
Cauchy (1789–1857)	Father: lawyer; brilliant; educated in classics and old languages; took refuge in country from French Revolution with circle of scholars.	During retreat father provided systematic, age-graded education to four children. Cauchy from age three. Contact as a young boy with Laplace and other French scholars in local intellectual circle with father.
Lobatchevsky (1792–1856)	Father: architect-surveyor; poor; ill. Foster father: surveyor; aided family; died when Lobatchevsky was five. Second son.	Mother, despite poverty, moved to Kazan to enter three sons in a good gymnasium at public expense, Lobatchevsky at eight, probably because of precocity. Sparse records.
Abel (1802–1829)	Father and grandfather: pastors. Father: science-education oriented; brilliant. Maternal aunt: well educated in music and literature. Second of six siblings.	Father educated Abel from three to thirteen (graded methods), with older brother; father loved to play with children. Aunt taught Abel to read at five. Prematurity brought undivided attention from mother during infancy.
Jacobi (1804–1851)	Father: banker. Wealthy, intellectual family. Uncle: math-classics educated. Second of three sons, one daughter.	Uncle educated him intensively in math and classics well enough to enter gymnasium at eleven. Quick mind, precocious.

Table 1. *(continued)*

Mathematician	Milieu	Special Early Experiences
Hamilton (1805–1865)	Father: well-educated. Uncle: clergyman; scholar in classics-old languages, as was aunt. Four sisters, one older, three younger. Lived with cousins from age three.	Uncle and aunt educated him systematically (including *many* ancient languages) from three until university at eighteen. Read fluently and knew arithmetic well at three, some geography at four; read Latin, Greek, and Hebrew well by five.
Galois (1811–1832)	Father and mother: classics scholars. Father ran school; wrote Latin and Greek verses.	Mother gave Galois intensive classics education (Latin, Greek) from preschool until entered Lycée at twelve. Early composed Latin and Greek verses for family celebrations.
Women		
Hypatia (370–415AD)	Father: math professor; ran scholarly university circle at museum.	Father tutored Hypatia comprehensively "from her earliest years" (Osen, 1974, p. 23), inspiring strong math-science interests.
Breteuil (1706–1749)	Father: judge; well-educated court figure. Mother: convent-educated. Renowned intellectual circle in home. Family friend: mathematician, who tutored her. Fifth of five siblings.	Father very early gave her fine classical education, strong in science and math. Very precocious, studious childhood. Spoke English and Italian fluently from childhood. Top calculation skills and memory. Rousseau may have tutored her at age six.
Agnesi (1718–1799)	Father: math professor; led circle of scholars in home. Mother: literate family. First of twenty-one siblings.	Educated informally from before age three or four and formally thereafter by tutors and parents, "who very carefully planned young girl's education" (Osen, 1974, p. 40) in math, science, and modern and old languages. Early child prodigy, speaking French by five and sight translating Greek and Latin by six.
Germain (1776–1831)	Father: deputy to estates general and director, Bank of France. Family: wealthy, educated, fine home library. Siblings?	No information before period of family social isolation during French Revolution, when began intensive self-study at age thirteen in family library, concentrating on math.
Somerville (1780–1872)	Father: admiral; avid reader; scientific florist. Mother: intellectual family; religious but indulgent. Older and younger brother and younger sister.	Mother taught Somerville to read through the Bible, probably during early years, and to read advanced material (*Pilgrim's Progress*) avidly by eight. Studied fauna and flora of Scottish coast from earliest years; father apparently stimulated.

Kovalevsky (1850–1891)	Father: well-educated general. Mother: intellectual. Nanny, tutors. Two grandfathers and uncle mathematicians. Older sister and younger brother.	Nanny told Kovalevsky fairy tales very early. Learned to read at five in family interaction. Math influences: grandfathers for models, early discussions of math with uncle, and calculus formulae on bedroom wall paper. Parents rejected her becoming a mathematician because she was a girl.
Noether (1882–1935)	Father: mathematics professor who conducted circle of math scholars in home. Mother: merchant family. Uncle: professor. Three younger brothers.	Father exercised "a strong influence on the early thinking of his children" (Osen, 1974, p. 142), of whom a younger brother and one of Noether's playmates became mathematicians. Early stimulated by father's math discussions. Quick mind.

Table 2. Starting Ages, Agents, and Domains of Special Early Stimulation and Early Intellectual Models for Great Men and Women Mathematicians

Mathematicians by Quality of Evidence	Special Early Stimulation						Early Intellectual Models[b]	
	Age	Agents[b]	Mu	Ma	Rd	La	General	Mathematics
Men								
Direct								
Descartes	3	FGmN	+	+	+	+	F	
Pascal	3	F	+	+	+	+	F	F
Newton	3	M	+[c]				MUGmSf	
Leibniz	5	F	+		+		FMGfO	
Monge	5	FO	+	+	+		FU	FU
Gauss	3	UMF	+	+	+		UFM	F
Cauchy	3	F	+	+	+	+	FO	O
Abel	3	FMA	+	+	+		FAM	
Hamilton	3	UA	+	+	+	+	UAF	
Indirect								
Euler	5	F	+	+	+[c]		FM[c]O	F
Lagrange	5		+[c]		+[c]	+[c]	FM[c]GfO	F
Laplace	5	U	+[c]	+[c]			U	U
Lobatchevsky	5	MFO	+[c]	+[c]			FOM[c]	FO
Jacobi	5	U	+	+	+[c]	+	UF	UF
Galois	5	MF[c]	+	+	+	+	MFGf	
Little Information								
Fermat							FMU	FU
Fourier								F
Poncelet							FFp	
Women								
Direct								
Hypatia	5	F	+	+	+	+	FO	FO
Agnesi	3	FM	+	+	+	+	FMO	FO
Somerville	5	FM	+		+		FM	
Kovalevsky	5	NFMO	+	+	+	+[c]	FMUON	UGfGfO
Indirect								
Breteuil	5	FO[c]	+	+	+[c]	+	FO	O
Noether	5	FO	+	+			FUO	FUO
Little Information								
Germain							F	F

[a] Mu = multiple, Ma = math, Rd = reading, La = foreign languages.
[b] F = father, M = mother, U = uncle, A = aunt, Gf = grandfather, Gm = grandmother, N = nurse, Sf = stepfather, Fp = foster parents, O = other.
[c] Seems probable.

ecologies. All except Fourier were reared with at least one educated close family member as an intellectual model. Fermat's father and uncle were merchants, his father also a consul, and his mother came from a highly educated family of magistrates. A complete library of French playwrights in the home of Poncelet's foster family would indicate intellectual models who might well have "seen to his earliest education" in a manner that would help account for how a boy of ten could come to read all the plays, supposedly on his own, and be advanced in primary school, as well as be able to dismantle and reassemble clocks. Similarly, Germain's option to withdraw to an extensive family library (uncommon for the era), while her father (a deputy of the estates-general and director of the Bank of France) discussed politics, is also an obvious marker of a rich intellectual milieu. Such withdrawal and steadfast perseverance to study mathematics on her own, in opposition to extraordinary parental pressures, moreover, depicts a confirmed, highly skilled reader whose pleasure and solace in books was long-standing, very possibly beginning in early childhood. Such backgrounds do not of course guarantee that special stimulation was experienced in their early years, but it is suggestive and certainly does not rule it out. This leaves us with Fourier.

Although apparently without intellectual family models beyond a master tailor father, his attendance at a small church school may well have begun during early childhood, following the frequent eighteenth-century practice (Daston, 1973). The later support of local patrons to attend a good military school (Herivel, 1975) because of his "quick mind" may also indicate an early school start. Not to be overlooked, however, is the fact that less educated families may well stimulate their children academically in the early years. Gauss's modestly educated parents and uncle clearly did so in reading and calculation, and Monge's storekeeper father apparently did so (the father wrote well) also, well enough to gain early admission for his three sons (all of whom became successful mathematicians) to an academic school (college); Monge, the eldest, when he was only five. Such practices among the less educated are not uncommon in our time (Durkin, 1966).

Presence of Intellectual Models. The number of intellectual models figuring in the lives of these great mathematicians underscores the frequent breadth of their cultural-intellectual background. All but five cases (4 men and 1 woman) are known to have been exposed to 2 or more intellectual models during early childhood, and in 3 of the cases, Descartes, Pascal, and Germain, the omission is undoubtedly one of information, not of fact. The kind of circles in which these families moved was replete with scholarly, intellectual associations, as much during their children's early as during their later development. At least 10 of the men and 5 of the women appear to have been actively involved in more or less formal adult intellectual circles quite early in life. Thus, a scholarly intellectual milieu of parents and their colleagues was generally available as a vital force for mental development throughout the formative years, greatly expanding the knowledge acquired through special early instruction. Just who were the agents of the special early stimulation programs? What types of concepts did they stimulate? And how did mathematics begin in some form?

Agents of Early Stimulation. The most frequent agent of instruction was the father (in 10 men and 6 women), as Table 2 shows, followed by the mother (5 men and 3 women, but sometimes jointly by the mother and the father). In only a single case (Galois), however, was the mother the chief agent, the one who assumed direct responsibility for the child's education throughout childhood, until he enrolled in school at age 12. An uncle was either the most important agent or an important agent in 4 cases and an aunt in 2, sometimes jointly or with the father. Descartes's nurse and grandmother may have served important stimulating functions through the exceptional care and attention they bestowed on him during his fragile infancy. This special attention seems to have engendered a degree of active curiosity that led the father to call Descartes his "little philosopher" and to respond with an extensive program of informal and formal instruction following the mother's death. Prematurity and fragility in infancy also appear to have played at least contributing roles in inducing the special attention of the mothers of Abel and Newton and probably Pascal. The contributions of the mother and various other family members are probably grossly understated in the limited records of biographers who often had little conception of the potentialities of stimulation, as compared to heredity, to influence mental development. Various clues suggest that Gauss, Hamilton, Leibniz, Agnesi, and Kovalevsky also probably began to experience special stimulation during infancy. What sorts of academic material did they use and what were their teaching strategies and methods?

The Curriculum. At least some evidence on the material taught can be found for all cases except for those in which information on their early lives is lacking (3 men, 1 woman), plus Newton. Broad strategies of instruction, embracing general knowledge and the three basic skills of reading writing, and arithmetic, were the most common fare (11 men and 5 women, plus 5 probable cases). In short, the basic elementary school curriculum was simply started early—but with important differences. Education was rooted in the classics, and Latin and Greek were frequent, because the scholarly knowledge of the day was largely written in those languages (Carr, 1929). Seven of the men and 3 of the women learned early to converse and study in those languages, but again this figure is undoubtedly underestimated. The 12 men and 4 women who definitely or probably began reading early almost certainly included additional ones who read early in Latin and Greek, though this is not always explicit, and the description of their early acquisition of foreign languages is sometimes ambiguous with regard to reading or merely speaking. Learning to recite passages and even compose prose or verse, as Galois did, was in any case a common practice. Early multilingual fluency in both modern and classical languages is reported for 10 of the 25 cases (7 men and 3 women), providing evidence in line with recent studies on the value of bilingual education in developing cognitive skills (Willig, 1985; Fowler, 1971).

Methods. As to their methods (not in Table 2), combinations of informal interaction, using age-graded material and styles (Descartes, Pascal, Leibniz, Gauss) were common, along with systematically planned programs and sometimes quite formal instruction. While information on methods used is limited, 11 men and 4 women had their early instruction initiated by the agent, while among 3 men and 4 women at least partially incidental approaches (such as initially responding to the child's demands, as Descartes's father did) were also reported. Except possibly for Gauss, however, in all cases where details are recorded, planned programs were invariably employed, once instruction was started. This pattern contrasts with my (Fowler, 1981) case study analysis of high-IQ children, in which about half the parents claimed not to have planned their children's intensive early stimulation. The latter figure is probably inflated, however, by the reluctance of parents in a modern context to be perceived as "pushing" their children. For the mathematicians, informal methods were indicated for 7 men and 6 women.

Early Stimulation in Mathematics. Some form of early special mathematical stimulation, usually number concepts and calculation skills, was indicated or inferrable in 12 men and 4 women (Table 2). Ten men and 6 women enjoyed the presence of skilled mathematicians in the family or milieu, sometimes formally as university professors or teachers (Hypatia, Agnesi, Noether, Laplace, Cauchy), sometimes as a strong interest (Pascal, Euler, Jacobi, Kovalevsky, Breteuil), sometimes as integral to their work (Lobatchevsky, Fermat, Lagrange, Germain, and possibly Monge), or sometimes in the form of demonstrated skills in calculation (the father of Gauss, who probably not coincidentally became a renowned mental calculator as well as conceptual mathematician). Did the remaining 4 men and 1 woman (Newton, Leibniz, Fourier, Poncelet, and Somerville) then come to greatness in mathematics without any apparent special early exposure to either stimulation or models in mathematics from any source?

The absence of direct evidence or the possibility of direct inference of early stimulation in math concepts does not mean that none occurred. As I have already noted, it seems inconceivable that Poncelet or Germain could have suddenly become avid scholars in middle childhood without well-founded early preparation. Quite possibly they were stimulated early in math as well as in reading and the humanities, as is suggested by Poncelet's strong mechanical interests and the mathematical competence of Germain's father as Director of the Bank of France. The same may be true of Newton, of whom we know only that his intellectual mother stimulated him in the first few years and not what she taught. While verbal stimulation was highly likely with an educated woman of the era, Newton's emerging preoccupation with mechanical inventions also suggests the possibility of early maternal attention to spatial and measurement activities, if not to number concepts themselves—not an improbability for a husbandless farm woman. Somerville's early years on the wild Scottish coast were full of opportunities to explore nature, stimulated by her naturalist-florist father to identify and classify the flora and fauna of the area. Poncelet, too, enjoyed extensive spatial experience through his endless opportunities to explore the countryside. Spatial skills have been widely seen as an important basis for the development of mathematics competence (Benbow and Stanley, 1983; Fennema and Sherman, 1977). The importance of spatial experience is seen also in the case of Monge, on whom both the father and uncle plied skilled manual trades (the uncle offered repair services in his hardware store). All three mathematical brothers are reported to have developed exceptional mechanical skills, apparently stemming from experience with their uncle's repair activities. Monge invented numerous devices, including a fire pump, by age twelve. But what of Fourier and Leibniz?

The likelihood of Fourier's starting early in the little church school (along with the possibility of early parental stimulation, as in the case of Gauss) has already been discussed, and math concepts would no doubt have been included. His tailor father would also have performed spatial manipulations and probably kept accounts, again both potentially good models for developing mathematics skills. There is no hint of mathematics in the early program of reading and history Leibniz was given by his father, but again, lack of information cannot be taken as negative evidence. The father's interest in an early start is in line with the accelerated general education practices of the era (for those who educated their children at all), which as we have seen ordinarily included mathematics. Thus, some combination of mathematics, calculation, and measurement concepts seems clearly to have formed part of the mathematician's special early experiences in most cases, and quite possibly in all cases.

But it is also true that the early stress on mathematics was not usually equal to the typically high stress on verbal skills. Pascal, Euler, Jacobi, Gauss, and possibly a few others were steeped in mathematics from the beginning, while the early instruction of Hamilton, Galois, Cauchy, and others, though including mathematics, was concentrated on the verbal world of reading, writing, foreign languages, and verbal communication and knowledge, especially in the classics. The early experiences of certain mathematicians like Somerville, Poncelet, Monge, Newton, and possibly others, moreover, apparently included less exposure to manipulating mathematics symbols than to spatial-mechanical experiences that influenced the form of their development in mathematics. And certain cases, notably Leibniz, may have received virtually no early exposure to mathematics symbols at all.

Does this variation suggest that early complex manipulations in the verbal domain can serve important functions for mathematics development? Can they perhaps even serve as a primary generative foundation adequate for later acquisition of complex, abstract competence in mathematics? If so, is this perhaps because mathematics and verbal symbol manipulations are organized in terms of similarly abstract and arbitrary representational symbols and highly logical and complex rule systems, making transfer from verbal to mathematics domains comparatively easy (Aiken, 1971; Fowler and Swenson, 1979)? What may be important is less the form of the notational system in which early stimulation occurs than the complexity and abstraction of the reasoning processes experienced.

Later Childhood Experiences. Despite their obvious importance, the later childhood experiences of these mathematicians need not occupy us more than to note the richness of their experiences, invariably directly concentrated in mathematics, of course, but usually broadly experienced across the fields of science and general knowledge and literature as well. Both men and women grew up in aspiring family milieux of educated models and rich intellectual associations, typically in the home, but sometimes more in school. All except Pascal received formal schooling, though sometimes after the early home programs were prolonged to the early teen years (Galois, Hamilton), and even he participated in intellectual circles outside the home, such as with renowned French scholars from age twelve on. All family ecologies were strongly supportive in one way or another, and in four cases, where families themselves lacked financial resources and social opportunities, the child's precocious abilities attracted the support of wealthy patrons or public aid (Laplace, Monge, Fourier, Lobatchevsky).

In addition to the various social barriers against careers for women, particularly in the sciences (for example, neither Russian nor German universities would admit women as mathematics students or appoint them math professors until very late in the nineteenth century), three of the women encountered strong career opposition from their families (Germain, Somerville, Kovalevsky), although only Somerville's parents failed to reverse their position eventually. Somerville depended on occasional mentors, persevering self-study, and the later support of a second husband. It is interesting that what families may do or make available in their children's early lives brings intellectual consequences families are not always prepared to support, as with these women. In addition, Abel and Euler had been originally destined for the ministry (like their fathers) but were given early academic instruction that led to passions for quite different life courses. Laplace may have followed a similar pattern. Newton had been slated to be a farmer. Family opposition was apparently never strong among the men mathematicians, however.

Mentors continued to feature in their later development. Many of the mathematicians encountered at least one great or at least perceptive-mathematics teacher who either stressed the conceptual rather than the typical rote memorization of the time or could at least recognize the importance of encouraging these precocious learners to pursue learning in their own manner, as in the case of Jacobi. The contribution of later mentors is not always clear, not only because of limited records but because, without exception, self-directed study, usually diverging considerably from standard curricula, marked the later developmental paths of all twenty-five of these exceptional mathematicians. Sometimes close relations with a highly skilled mathematical schoolmate served a mentor function (as in the cases of Descartes, Kovalevsky, probably Germain, and the three Monge brothers, who often studied together).

Model for Developmental Learning of Mathematics Competence. The developmental courses of these mathematicians were at once similar and divergent. A general model of the course they followed probably begins in early infancy with unusual adult attention involving language and cognitive skills. We have evidence of this in at least nine cases. The resulting accelerated speech, keen intellectual curiousity, and problem-solving and reasoning skills, no doubt reflecting original potential as well, created family expectations of intellectual promise (Bloom, 1982, refers to them as markers). These expectations then led one or more family members to provide special academic instruction, beginning in late infancy or early childhood (between two and five). Over the ensuing early years, the cumulative effects of the infants' attention and intensive early childhood program of abstract symbol manipulation skills and complex concepts gradually generated a highly autonomous cognitive processing system. This system led the young children to actively seek out and eventually to begin to create increasingly complex material on their own, making use of the intellectual resources of various special mentors whose attention these "gifted" systems attracted along the way.

Nevertheless, later development continued the same intensive program of stimulation (usually now in school) and encountered special mentors, but now more and more combined with intensive self-directed study and sooner or later almost entirely centered on mathematics. This outline for the development of exceptional competence in mathematics in many ways paralleled the development of high competence in literary, scientific, and other fields noted earlier. It also shared many of the elements of the investigator's model for development identified in Terman's high-IQ children (Fowler, 1981).

Chief among the variations in developmental courses were the accidents of prematurity, poor infant health, or parental death (Newton's father) that called up exceptional care in infancy and the early presence or absence of highly skilled mathematics teachers (compare Feldman, 1980). The latter variation influenced how much mathematics was infused in the preschool curriculum and the timing of when mathematics became the central focus of mental development. This variation provided support for the hypothesis that early complex stimulation in verbal symbols may adequately generate a cognitive processing system capable of assimilating complex competence in mathematics at later points in development—even though some mathematics material may have formed part of the early curriculum in all cases. Other variations included who played the role of chief agent of instruction, the degree of initiative assumed by the agent in planning the instruction, the degree of informality or formality employed, and for the women mathematicians especially, the magnitude of the social barriers they had to surmount to pursue development and a career in mathematics.

Summary and Conclusions

If we consider the development of these great mathematicians, it would appear that there were certain constants, serving as developmental prerequisites, that marked their pathways, but that these constants assumed alternative forms. Each constant constituted a major source of cognitive stimulation that shaped the potentials of these individuals to develop exceptional competence in mathematics. Though promising, given the regularity with which these constants are found and the absence of negative evidence, the sparseness of evidence in certain cases dictates that these constants must still be treated with tentativeness.

The first apparent constant was the experience of special cognitive stimulation in early childhood (at least by age five and typically earlier). This varied in terms of the agents (father, mother, uncle, and so on), the degree of planning (highly planned versus partly incidental to child's demands), the methods (formal or informal), and the combination of domains stimulated (verbal—early reading, multiple languages; mathematical; spatial). But because complex verbal concepts were apparently invariably stressed while mathematics concepts were not, the verbal medium can apparently serve adequately for establishing the potential for acquiring skill in manipulating abstract symbols in other domains. Thus, verbal skills may generalize later to foster competence in reasoning with the similarly but even more abstract symbols of mathematics in cases where little or no stimulation in mathematics itself occurs during early development.

A second constant was the presence of intellectual models from earliest childhood, but again these varied from the highly educated parents of Cauchy and Pascal to the self-educated uncle and the modestly educated but skill-focused parents of Gauss, who were yet adequate for establishing a good cognitive foundation. The domains of intellectual models also varied. While most of the significant figures were highly skilled in verbal skills and knowledge, especially in the classics and languages, many of the mathematicians were also exposed early to mathematics models, and eventually all encountered models important for their development in mathematics.

A third constant was the successful generation of self-propelled cognitive learning systems during early childhood. In all cases, the early cognitive stimulation was evidently sufficient to induce a passion and skill for learning that led the child to master increasingly complex material, sometimes with little aid and considerable opposition (Somerville, Germain, Kovalevsky). One may hypothesize that a common thread of the different forms, agents, and methods was a quality, intensity, and complexity of stimulation sufficient to produce a crucial transformation in the character of the young child's modes of cognitive functioning. The emergent cognitive system formed a complex foundation of knowledge, motivation, and above all strategies and autonomy in problem solving adequate to maintain complex learning in the same direction with minimal adult guidance.

Additional constants applied to later development. Thus, a fourth constant was the regularity with which the emerging, self-propelled cognitive system served a social reinforcement function. In case after case, the young child's developing skills were early labeled precocious, independent, and reflective. Once socially identified, other agents besides the original stimulating agents in the family—teachers, friends, and sponsors—mentors of all kinds would at various points further reinforce the direction and intensity of the child's increasingly self-motivated development. Such reinforcements included furnishing special guidance or encouragement, or exercising influence to enable the youngster to obtain advanced knowledge and schooling, as for example in the cases of Monge and Fourier for schooling and of Leibniz for obtaining through a family friend's intervention free access to the valuable library of his father on the latter's death (apparently a privilege for a young child in those days). All mathematicians continued to pursue intensive formal schooling throughout childhood and youth, though in some cases at home until the teen years (Galois, Hamilton) or throughout childhood (Pascal)—in all cases combined with intensive self-directed study. Intense intellectual exchange with mentors was also a constant but took the form of either special teachers (most frequent) or mathematically skilled schoolmates, scholars, friends, or even a spouse (Somerville).

High concentration and skill in mathematics was obviously still another constant, but the developmental timing was spread across a broad age span. These ranged from the high interest of Pascal and Gauss from their earliest years, through the gradual coming to math of Kovalevsky from an accumulation of influences (multiple family mathematics models, mathematics wallpaper in the bedroom, discussions with a mathematical uncle, and a mathematics student who admired her competence), to the later emphasis on mathematics over classics of Hamilton, Lagrange, and others, during youth. These findings compare closely with those of Bloom (1985) and his associates on the development patterns of a sample of contemporary world-class mathematicians. They match the frequent early stress on complex verbal processes and the wide age variation of beginning concentration on math. They may differ, however, in the frequency with which the earlier great mathematicians continued to engage in a rich variety of fields, especially languages and the classics, of which there is no mention in Bloom's group. Does this reflect the increasing specialization of our era?

It is not surprising that the later childhood of mathematicians is packed with rich mathematical experiences, in the form of formal schooling, encounters with mentors, and above all intensive self-directed study. The issue here, however, is not whether such later experiences are essential for the development of exceptional competence. The regularity with which they occur would indicate that they are. The concern here, rather, is whether such later technical concentration can be constructed on an ordinary foundation of early childhood competencies. On this count the evidence, though not definitive, strongly suggests that the early establishment of a complex mental foundation is as vital to exceptional adult competence in mathematics as the later mastery experiences.

The course of development for exceptional competence in mathematics in thus constructed of a rich cognitive foundation, apparently formed starting in infancy through unusually complex cognitive stimulation with abstract symbols, principally in the verbal medium. This early established cognitive system soon itself becomes a major source of stimulation for the further development of exceptional competence, now increasingly (if not already) centered in mathematics, compounding the strength of development attained through continuing intensive exposure to complex material, through schooling, and through the additional mentors the child's rapidly expanding talents attract.

Bibliography

Alexandrov, P. C. *Nicolai Ivanovich Lobatchevski.* Moscow: Gosudarstvennoe Eezdatelstvo, 1943.

Anzoletti, L. *Maria Gaetana Agnesi.* Milano: Tipografia Editrice L. F. Cogliati, 1900.

Arago, M. *Biographie de Gaspard Monge.* Smith Collection, unpublished documents, Columbia University Library, 1846.

Aubry, P. V. *Monge: Le savant ami de Napoléon Bonaparte.* Paris: Gauthier-Villars, 1954.

Baillet, A. *Vie de Monsieur Descartes*. Paris: Collection "Grandeurs," La Table Ronde, 1691.

Bertrand, J. *Blaise Pascal*. Paris: Calman Lévy, 1891.

Bjerknes, C.-A. *Niels-Henrik Abel: Tableau de sa vie et de son action scientifique*. Paris: Gauthier-Villars, 1885.

Bogolubov, A. N. *Gaspar Monge*. Moscow: Eesdatelstvo "Nauka," 1978.

Brewer, J. W., and Smith, M. K. *Emmy Noether: A Tribute to Her Life and Work*. New York: Marcel Dekker, 1981.

Brewster, D. *Memoirs of the Life, Writings, and Discoveries of Sir Issac Newton*. Edinburgh: Thomas Constable and Co., 1855.

Browne, P. Mrs. *Somerville and Mary Carpenter*. London: Cassel, 1887.

Bucciarelli, L. L., and Dworsky, N. *Sophie Germain*. Boston, Reidel, 1980.

Bühler, W. K. *Gauss: A Biographical Study*. New York: Springer-Verlag, 1981.

Burckhardt, F. *Die Basler Mathematiker: Daniel Bernoulli und Leonhard Euler*. Basel: H. Georg's, 1884.

Burzio, F. *Lagrange*. Torino: Unione Tipographco-editrice Torinese, 1942.

Caillet, E. *Pascal: The Emergence of Genius*. (2nd ed.) New York: Harper & Row, 1961.

David, F. N. "Some Notes on Laplace." In J. Neyman and L. M. LeCam (Eds.) *Bernoulli, Bayes, Laplace*. New York: Springer-Verlag, 1965.

Dewey, J. *Leibniz's New Essays Concerning Human Understanding: A Critical Exposition*. Chicago: Scott, Foresman, 1902.

Dick, A. *Emmy Noether: 1882-1935*. Boston: Birkhäuser, 1981.

Dirichlet, L. "Gedächtnissrede auf Carl Gustav Jacob Jacobi." In C. W. Borchardt (Ed.), *C. G. J. Jacobi's Gesammelte Werke*. Berlin: Verlag von G. Reimer, 1881.

Dunnington, G. W. *Carl Friedrich Gauss: Titan of Science*. New York: Exposition Press, 1955.

Dupuy, P. *La Vie d'Evariste Galois*. Paris: Cahiers de la Quinzaine, 1903.

Ferval, C. *Madame du Châtelet: Une maîtresse de Voltaire*. Paris: Librairie Arthéme Fayard, 1948.

Forti, C. A. *Intorno alla vita e alle opere di Luigi Lagrange*. Pisa: Dalla Tipografia Nistri, 1868.

Gillispie, C. C. (Ed.). *Dictionary of Scientific Biography*. New York: Scribner's, 1970-1976.

Grattan-Guiness, I. *Joseph Fourier: 1768-1830*. Cambridge, Mass.: The MIT Press, 1972.

Graves, R. P. *Life of Sir William Rowan Hamilton*. Dublin: Hodges, Figgis & Co., 1882.

Guitton, J. *Génie de Pascal*. Paris: Aubier, 1962.

Haldane, E. S. *Descartes: His Life and Times*. London: John Murray, 1905.

Hall, T. *Carl Friedrich Gauss*. Cambridge, Mass.: The MIT Press, 1970.

Hamel, F. *An Eighteenth-Century Marquise: A Study of Emilie du Châtelet and Her Times*. New York: James Pott, 1911.

Hankins, T. L. *Sir William Rowan Hamilton*. Baltimore, Md.: Johns Hopkins University Press, 1980.

Hubbard, E. *Little Journeys to the Homes of Great Teachers: Hypatia*. East Aurora, N.Y.: The Roycrofters, 1908.

Itard, J. *Pierre Fermat*. Basel: Birkhäuser, 1950.

Juge-Chapsal, C. *Tricentenaire de la mort de Blaise Pascal*. Clermont-Ferrand, France: Editions G. de Bussac, 1962.

Kagan, B. F. *Lobatchevsky*. Moscow: Academy of Science, USSR, 1948.

Keeling, S. V. *Descartes*. London: Oxford University Press, 1968.

Koenigsberger, L. *Carl Gustav Jacob Jacobi.* Leipzig: Druck und Verlag von B. G. Teubner, 1904.

Kollros, L. *Evariste Galois.* Basel: Birkhäuser, 1949.

Kusch, E. *C. G. J. Jacobi und Helmholtz auf dem Gymnasium.* Potsdam: Kramer'sche Buchdruckerei (Paul Brandt), 1896.

Kuznetsov, B. G. *Lomonosov, Lobachevsky, Mendeleyev: Ocherky, jisni e meerovozreneya.* Moscow: Academy of Science, USSR, 1945.

Launay, L. de. *Monge: Fondateur de l'école polytechnique.* Paris: Editions Pierre Roger, 1935.

Leffler, A. C. *Sonya Kovalevsky: Her Recollections of Childhood, with a Biography.* New York: Century, 1895.

Lewis, G. *Réne Descartes: Français, philosophe.* Paris: Mame, 1953.

Mackie, J. M. *Life of Leibniz.* Boston: Gould, Kendall, & Lincoln, 1845.

Mahaffy, J. P. *Descartes.* Edinburgh: William Blackwood & Sons, 1880.

Mahoney, M. S. *The Mathematical Career of Pierre de Fermat.* Princeton, N. J.: Princeton University Press, 1973.

Manuel, F. E. *A Portrait of Isaac Newton.* Cambridge, Mass.: Harvard University Press, 1968.

Maurel, A. *La Marquise du Châtelet: Une amie de Voltaire.* Paris: Hachette, 1930.

Mersbach, U. C. "Emmy Noether: Historical Context." In B. Srinivasan and J. Sally (Eds.), *Emmy Noether in Bryn Mawr.* New York: Springer-Verlag, 1983.

Merz, J. T. *Leibniz.* Edinburgh: William Blackwood & Sons, 1907.

Mesnard, J. (Ed.). *Blaise Pascal: Oeuvres complètes.* Bruges: Edition du Tricentenaire, 1964.

Meyer, W. A. *Hypatia von Alexandria.* Heidelberg: George Weiss, 1886.

Mitford, N. *Voltaire in Love.* London: Hamish Hamilton, 1957.

Mittag-Leffler, G. *Neils Henrik Abel.* Paris: La Revue du Mois, 1907.

More, L. T. *Isaac Newton: A Biography.* New York: Scribner's, 1934.

Morgan, A. de. *Essays on the Life and Work of Newton.* Chicago: Open Court, 1914.

Morton, E. J. C. *Heroes of Science: Astronomers.* London: Society for Promoting Christian Knowledge, 1882.

Mozans, H. J. *Woman in Science.* Cambridge, Mass.: The MIT Press, 1974.

Noether, E. P., and Gottfried, E. "Emmy Noether in Erlangen and Göttingen." In B. Srinivasan and J. Sally (Eds.), *Emmy Noether in Bryn Mawr.* New York: Springer-Verlag, 1983.

Ore, O. *Niels Henrik Abel: Mathematician Extraordinary.* Minneapolis: University of Minnesota Press, 1957.

Pearl, L. *Descartes.* Boston: Twayne Publishers, 1977.

Périer, G. *The Life of Pascal with his Letters Relating to the Jesuits.* Vol. 1: *The Life of Mr. Pascal: Written by His Sister, Madam Périer.* (W. A., Trans.) London: Bettenham, 1744.

Pesloüan, C. L. de. *N.-H. Abel: Sa vie et son oeuvre.* Paris: Gauthier-Villars, 1906.

Pogrebiski, E. B. *Gottfried William Leibniz.* Moscow: Eezapalstvo Nauka, 1971.

Polubarinova-Kochina, P. *Sophia Vasilyevna Kovalevskaya: Her Life and Work.* Moscow: Foreign Language Publishing House, 1957.

Rogers, H. *Essays: Critical and Biographical.* London: Longmans, Green, 1874.

Serret, M.J.-A. de (Ed.). *Oeuvres de Lagrange.* Paris: Gauthier-Villars, 1867.

Smith, D. E. *Portraits of Eminent Mathematicians, with Brief Biographical Sketches.* New York: Scripta Mathematica, 1938.

Somerville, M. (Ed.). *Personal Recollections of Mary Somerville.* Boston: Roberts Brothers, 1874.

Taton, R. *Gaspard Monge.* Basel: Birkhäuser, 1950.
Taton, R. "Jean Victor Poncelet." In C. C. Gillispie (Ed.), *Dictionary of Scientific Biography,* vol. 11. New York: Scribner's, 1976.
Tribout, H. *Un grand savant: Le Général Jean-Victor Poncelet.* Paris: Librairie Georges Saffroy, 1936.
Vaillot, R. *Madame du Châtelet.* Paris: Albin Michel, 1978.
Valson, C.-A. *La vie et les travaux du Baron Cauchy.* Paris: Gauthier-Villars, 1868.
Vrooman, J. R. *René Descartes: A Biography.* New York: Putnam, 1970.
Waltershausen, W. S. von. *Gauss: A memorial.* Leipzig: S. Hirzel, 1856.
Westfall, R. S. *Never at Rest: A Biography of Isaac Newton.* Cambridge, England: Cambridge University Press, 1980.

References

Aiken, L. R. "Verbal Factors in Mathematics Learning: A Review of Research." *Journal for Research in Mathematics Education,* 1971, *2,* 304-313.
Bell, E. T. *Men of Mathematics.* New York: Simon & Schuster, 1965.
Benbow, C., and Stanley, J. "Sex Differences in Mathematical Reasoning: More Facts." *Science,* 1983, *222,* 1029-1031.
Bennett, B. "The Childhood Environments of Famous Artists." Unpublished manuscript, Ontario Institute for Studies in Education, Toronto, 1967.
Bloom, B. S. "The Role of Gifts and Markers in the Development of Talent." *Exceptional Children,* 1982, *48,* 510-522.
Bloom, B. S. (Ed.) *Developing Talent in Young People.* New York: Ballantine, 1985.
Carr, H. W. *Leibniz.* London: E. Benn, 1929.
Cox, C. M. *The Early Mental Traits of Three Hundred Geniuses.* Vol. 2: *Genetic Studies in Genius.* Stanford, Calif.: Stanford University Press, 1926.
Daston, L. J. "Evariste Galois and the French Mathematical Community." Unpublished honors thesis, Department of History of Science, Harvard University, 1973.
Dupin, C. *Essai historique sur les services et les travaux scientifique de Gaspard Monge.* Paris: Bachelier, Libraire, Quai des Augustins, 1819.
Durbach, E. Untitled seminar paper on the development of five eminent playwrights, Ontario Institute for Studies in Education, Toronto, 1979.
Durkin, D. *Children Who Read Early.* New York: Teachers College Press, Columbia University, 1966.
Earle, A. M. *Child Life in Colonial Days.* Folcroft, Pa.: Folcroft Library Editions, 1974.
Este, H. "Five Victorian Novelists in the Making: Their Early and Middle Childhood Years." Unpublished manuscript, Ontario Institute for Studies in Education, Toronto, 1979.
Feldman, D. H. *Beyond Universals in Cognitive Development.* Norwood, N.J.: Ablex, 1980.
Fennema, E., and Sherman, J. "Sex-Related Differences in Mathematics Achievement, Spatial Visualization, and Affective Factors." *American Educational Research Journal,* 1977, *14,* 51-71.
Fowler, W. "Cognitive Learning in Infancy and Early Childhood." *Psychological Bulletin,* 1962, *59,* 116-152.
Fowler, W. "Cognitive Baselines in Early Childhood: Developmental Learning and Differentiation of Competence Rule Systems." In J. Hellmuth (Ed.), *Cognitive Studies.* Vol. 2: *Cognitive Deficits.* New York: Brunner/Mazel, 1971.
Fowler, W. "Sequence and Styles in Cognitive Development." In I. C. Uzgiris and F. Weizmann (Eds.), *The Structure of Experience.* New York: Plenum, 1977.

Fowler, W. "Cognitive Differentiation and Developmental Learning." In H. W. Reese and L. P. Lipsitt (Eds.), *Advances in Child Development and Behavior, Vol. 15.* New York: Academic Press, 1980.

Fowler, W. "Case Studies of Cognitive Precocity: The Role of Exogenous and Endogenous Stimulation in Early Mental Development." *Journal of Applied Developmental Psychology,* 1981, *2,* 319-367.

Fowler, W. *Potentials of Childhood.* Lexington, Mass.: Lexington Books, 1983.

Fowler, W., and Swenson, A. "The Influence of Early Language Stimulation on Development: Four Studies." *Genetic Psychology Monographs,* 1979, *100,* 73-109.

Fuss, N. "Eloge de Léonard Euler." In *Oeuvres Complètes de L. Euler.* Tome 1: *Lettres à une princesse d'allemagne.* Bruxelles: Etablissement geographique près la porte de Flandre, 1839.

Galton, F. *Inquiries into Human Faculty and its Development.* London: Dent, 1907.

Gardner, H. *Frames of Mind: The Theory of Multiple Intelligences.* New York: Basic Books, 1983.

Gottfried, A. W. (Ed.). *Home Environment and Early Cognitive Development: Longitudinal Research.* New York: Academic Press, 1984.

Herivel, J. *Joseph Fourier: The Man and Physicist.* Oxford: Clarendon, 1975.

Hunt, J. M. *Intelligence and Experience.* New York: Ronald Press, 1961.

Lazar, I., and Darlington, R. B. "Lasting Effects of Early Education: A Report from the Consortium for Longitudinal Studies." *Monographs of the Society for Research in Child Development,* 1982, *47* (entire serial no. 195).

Osen, L. M. *Women in Mathematics.* Cambridge, Mass.: The MIT Press, 1974.

Pasquier, L.-G. du. *Léonard Euler et ses amis.* Paris: Librairie Scientifique J. Herman, 1927.

Root, W. T. "A Socio-Psychological Study of Fifty-Three Supernormal Children." *Psychological Monographs,* 1921, *29* (entire no. 133).

Spiess, O. *Leonhard Euler.* Leipzig: Von Huber & Co., 1929.

Terman, L. M. *The Intelligence of School Children.* Boston: Houghton Mifflin, 1919.

Terman, L. M. *Genetic Studies of Genius.* Vol. 1. *Mental and Physical Traits of a Thousand Gifted Children.* Stanford, Calif.: Stanford University Press, 1925.

Tetroe, J. "A Case Study of the Early Experience of Five Eminent Scientists." Unpublished manuscript, Ontario Institute for Studies in Education, Toronto, 1979.

Virey, J. J., and Potel (no initials). *Précis historique sur la vie et la mort de Joseph-Louis Lagrange.* Paris: Ve. Courcier, 1813.

Walberg, H. J. (Ed.). *Educational Environments and Effects.* Berkeley, Calif.: McCutchan, 1979.

Willig, A. C. "A Meta-Analysis of Selected Studies on the Effectiveness of Bilingual Education." *Review of Educational Research,* 1985, *55,* 269-317.

William Fowler, for many years a professor of applied psychology at the Ontario Institute for Studies in Education at the University of Toronto, is now a visiting research scientists in the Eliot-Pearson Department of Child Study at Tufts University and director of the Center for Early Learning and Child Care in Cambridge. His interests include the study of early experience, socialization, day care, and cognitive development.

Students in Japanese culture are introduced to learning situations
in structured ways that develop young children's control of their
learning behavior earlier than is
typical in the West.

Training Learning Skills and Attitudes in Japanese Early Educational Settings

Lois Peak

It is a commonly agreed in the comparative study of education and child development that cultural and environmental influences play an important role in determining both the abilities that children develop and the rate at which they achieve competence. Cultures that require children to master the skills required of daily life encourage the early development of complex skills that adults in other cultures might assume to be beyond a given age group's capabilities. A classic example is Margaret Mead's description of the degree of competence in canoeing and swimming that was achieved by five- and six-year-old children among the Manus of New Guinea. Because the Manus lived in houses raised on stilts above the water of a tidal lagoon, water was a more salient aspect of their environment than dry land. Exposed from infancy to swimming as an everyday means of locomotion, children quickly mastered the abilities necessary to life in this environment.

Field research for this chapter was generously supported by a Japan Foundation Fellowship and a Sinclair Kennedy Travelling Fellowship from Harvard University. I am indebted to Robert LeVine, William Fowler, and Hideo Kojima for their comments on earlier versions of the paper.

W. Fowler (Ed.). *Early Experience and the Development of Competence.*
New Directions for Child Development, no. 32. San Francisco: Jossey-Bass, June 1986.

111

A child's knowledge of a canoe is considered adequate if he (or she) can balance himself, feet planted on the two narrow (one inch) rims and punt the canoe with accuracy, paddle well enough to steer through a mild gale, run the canoe accurately under a house without jamming the outrigger, extricate a canoe from a flotilla of canoes crowded about a house platform or the edge of an islet, and bail out a canoe by a deft backward and forward movement which dips the bow and stern alternately. Understanding of the sea includes swimming, diving, swimming under water, and a knowledge of how to get water out of nose and throat by leaning the head forward and striking the back of the neck. Children of between five and six have mastered these necessary departments (Mead, 1975, p. 35).

Western students of child development who rarely spend significant amounts of time in cultures outside of the industrialized West have few opportunities to be so graphically reminded of the central role of environmental influence and cultural expectations in shaping the development of early abilities. In studying the progress of children developing within our own familiar cultural environment, we often imagine that the rates of development typical of children in this particular culture reflect pan-human age-related competencies rather than the priorities and environmental demands of our own culture. Although the Manus case represents the early development of a largely physical ability in response to environmental demands, the development of more abstract cognitive abilities is also considerably influenced by the cultural environment. Gardner (1983) has recently presented detailed evidence on the interrelationship of cultural expectations and priorities and the development and selection of a broad range of human abilities.

As LeVine (1980) has observed, without the perspective gained by evidence concerning child development in other cultures, Western educators and psychologists run the risk of elevating Western folk assumptions about children's learning potential to the level of academic theory. Recommendations concerning age-appropriate learning activities, appropriate methods of teaching preschool children, and the proper goals of early education can thus become limited to a narrow range of alternatives derived largely from commonplace Western cultural assumptions and folk practices.

Japanese early educational beliefs and practices present an interesting case study for consideration from this point of view. As a fully modern, industrialized society that has received a substantial educational influence from the West, the overall structure and content of the formal educational system resembles that of the United States (Vogel, 1979). However, closer investigation reveals that the familiar external appearances conceal very different beliefs and practices that are deeply rooted in a highly sophisticated non-Western cultural and historical educational tradition. Modern Japanese children's superior performance on international tests of mathematics and science achievement (Comber and Keeves, 1973; Husen, 1967; Stigler and others, 1983) demonstrates that these different educational beliefs and practices are also associated with high competence in academic subjects and abilities relevant to classroom learning.

This chapter focuses on one aspect of the Japanese educational approach—the inculcation of basic learning skills and attitudes in novice learners, particularly training that develops basic cognitive support skills in early learning situations. This topic is particularly relevant to the discussion of the role of early experience in the development of competence for two reasons. First, this careful basic training in learning strategies and consequent thorough, reflective approach to learning tasks has been cited by Japanese psychologists (Kojima, 1985; Nagano, 1983) as an important ingredient in Japanese children's educational success. Second, the goals of this training and the manner in which it is carried out are foreign to American cultural beliefs about appropriate educational goals and teaching methods for preschool-age children. For these reasons it may spark reflection on our cultural assumptions concerning early education.

The data presented in this chapter were collected in 1983 and 1984, during eighteen months of ethnographic fieldwork in Japanese early learning environments such as preschools, various types of enrichment lessons, and first grades. Data were collected through intensive classroom observation, teacher interviews, and curriculum analysis during the first three months of the school year in each of two preschools, four first-grade classrooms, and one program of early music instruction. Supplementary interviews with principals and parents, questionnaires, analysis of popular books and magazines about early education, and briefer observation of a broad sample of other preschools, first grades, and other enrichment lessons were also conducted.

Introduction of Novice Students to Learning Situations

Both traditional and contemporary Japanese education place an extremely high priority on careful structuring of novice students' introduction to learning situations. Typically, the period of transition from initial applicant to fully accepted beginning student is considerably protracted, encompassing several months or more. During this period the new student undergoes systematic training in the basic attitudes and cognitive support skills fundamental to the medium to be learned. This preliminary training requires a long period of diligent study and thorough mastery of precisely defined basic routines before the student is allowed to engage in the medium itself. This training is combined with a calculated arousal of the learner's motivation to study and a training in concentration and self-monitoring skills.

The training involved in this preparatory period shares some similarity to the introduction of new students to learning situations the world over. However, the sophistication and detail of the procedures used in the Japanese case, their pervasiveness throughout a broad range of traditional and modern educational settings, and the unassuming ease with which they are used by even the pedagogically naive Japanese point to a highly elaborated indigenous cultural structuring of the educational process. Typically, these techniques are a part of the training of novice learners of any age in a broad range of settings, such as the induction of new employees into Japanese banks (Rohlen, 1974), studying traditional archery (Herrigel, 1953), and entering the first grade of public school (Taniuchi, 1985a). However, the techniques are more clearly defined and heavily emphasized in the teaching of very inexperienced learners such as preschool children. Across a broad range of different types of early learning environments, the following training practices were universally observed during the initial period of induction into the learning situation:

- Calculated arousal of learner motivation to acquire a specific skill and to become a member of its social setting
- Repeated practice of precisely defined basic component routines until they become automatic
- Development of self-monitoring of learning performance.

Japanese teachers and parents believe that careful establishment of these habits and attitudes is the first requirement for minimum teachability and one of the most important determinants of future success in learning endeavors. In all settings studied, the presentation of regular curriculum content is delayed for one to six months until students are judged to have developed the appropriate basic attitudes and habits. Once these are established, however, teaching shifts to an increasingly straightforward and rapid presentation of curriculum content with minimal need to slow the pace of instruction for the slow learner.

The effectiveness of these practices is evident in comparative studies of both Japanese children's approach to learning tasks and studies of classroom discipline. Salkind, Kojima, and Zelniker (1978) report that five- to seven-year-old Japanese children are significantly more reflective and more accurate than either American or Israeli children on tests of cognitive style such as the Matching Familiar Figures Test. This test requires children to identify which of six slightly different pictures exactly matches a certain model picture, making careful, repeated comparison of one picture after another before forming a judgment. Although at ages five, six, and seven, Japanese children are the slowest and most careful of the three groups, by age ten they have become faster than American or Israeli children. Japanese children make the fewest errors at all ages, until a measurement ceiling effect is reached at age eight among Japanese and at age ten among American and Israeli children. These results exemplify Japanese teachers' emphasis on a slow, careful approach to learning tasks during the early years that speeds up as children acquire facility and confidence.

Careful training in learning routines and development of concentration skills also pay off in better classroom management and less wasting of teaching time through student inattention and teacher attempts to reestablish order. Stevenson (1985) reports that Japanese first-grade children attend to the teacher when he or she is speaking better than their American counterparts (60 percent of the time as opposed to 45 percent) and display inappropriate behavior less frequently (12 percent of the time as opposed to 20 percent). This better classroom discipline, combined with more efficient routines for managing transitions between activities, allows Japanese teachers to spend almost 50 percent more time per hour imparting information. A few months of extra effort at the beginning of first grade appear to produce considerable benefits in making Japanese students both more attentive and easier to manage.

How is this initial training in learning skills and attitudes accomplished? This chapter describes the process using examples from both modern, formal early learning situations, such as preschool and first grade, and a more traditionally structured, informal setting, such as the Suzuki method of music instruction. In fact, the Suzuki method is a good case study for examining this training process because it exhibits in simple, straightforward form the cultural beliefs and practices used to develop proper learning skills and attitudes in other Japanese early educational settings. In addition, its similarity to traditional Japanese methods of teaching and learning (Taniuchi, 1985b), its relatively discrete focus of instruction, and its individual approach make it an ideal prototype against which to compare the more complex and diverse practices of Japanese preschools and elementary schools.

Before focusing in detail on the process by which these various early learning situations train novice students in basic learning skills and attitudes, a brief description of the Suzuki method is in order. The Suzuki method is a system of teaching musical instruments to children founded by Shinichi Suzuki, a Japanese violinist. Developed shortly after World War II according to very traditional Japanese patterns of teaching and learning, it has now been adopted in somewhat modified form in twenty-three other countries, chiefly in North America and Europe. Children begin lessons very early, usually during their third year, using instruments that have been scaled down or modified in size. Initially, students learn the classical musical repertoire solely by listening to records at home, in the same manner in which they acquire their native language. The child's mother is the central figure in the learning process, and the teacher's task is to teach the mother how to train her own child at home. Mothers study the instrument themselves in the beginning stages, starting lessons a few weeks before the child. They attend all lessons and lead all home practice sessions according to the teacher's directions until the child reaches upper elementary school age, at which time responsibility is gradually shifted to the child. Although most families in the program have had no prior musical background, children's progress is usually surprisingly rapid, and students are quickly able to play a difficult professional repertoire. Average violin students master Vivaldi concertos at age seven or eight and Mozart concertos at age ten or eleven. Faster students perform these works at age five or eight, respectively.

Arousing Learner Motivation. The manner in which a prospective Suzuki student is inducted into the lesson process exemplifies the Japanese practice of calculated inflation of learner motivation for a considerable period before training begins. When new students arrive to request piano or violin lessons, they and their mothers meet with the teacher, who describes the method and assigns them to a class of four or five other recent beginners and their mothers. For the first month or more the child and mother come once or twice a week and observe the other children's lessons and group activities, meanwhile listening daily at home to a recording of the first songs in the repertoire. As the child and the mother watch from the back of the room, the teacher and other mothers combine in telling the new student how much fun it is to learn to play the piano. The mother explains that if the child is very good, he or she may someday be allowed to join in the fun.

Once the child's interest has been visibly aroused, the *mother* begins lessons and daily home practice sessions. The child is required to wait a few weeks longer, watching alone from the back of the room during weekly group lessons and hearing and seeing the mother practice at home the same exercises that the child will soon learn. At this point, it is a rare child who does not daily beg to be allowed to practice the piano, too. When the mother and teacher see that the child's motivation is at a fever pitch, the first lessons begin.

This period of observation is the time-honored *minarai kikan,* or period of learning through watching, so typical of such varied Japanese educational and social institutions as Zen temples, junior high school tennis clubs, and salaried employment. In the Suzuki method, the goal of this preliminary period is obviously to awaken in the child a sufficiently high level of motivation that he or she is willing to undertake the difficult process of daily coaxing the fingers and body to learn the new and difficult combinations that constitute learning to play an instrument. However, interviews with master teachers revealed that they also have a less obvious goal in mind. The observation period continues not only until motivation is sufficiently aroused but until the child has become able to listen quietly and attentively to three or four consecutive lessons and can understand that the lesson situation is one in which quiet focusing of attention is required. This step may take anywhere from three to twelve weeks, depending on the age and personality of the child. Once the child has developed the ability to listen quietly, the first lesson in arousing motivation and training concentration has been accomplished.

In preschools and elementary schools, this period takes the form of several occasions on which incoming students are invited to observe the life of the school and see the older students in action. The incoming students are treated as special guests, and they watch from the sidelines at the yearly sports day and are invited to meet the teachers and older students, sit in the desks, and see their future classroom several weeks before school begins. Teachers and older students welcome the prospective students individually and give the children handmade gifts. As the first day of school approaches, new students receive uniforms or other identical clothing and regulation equipment that clearly mark their new status as members not only of a given school and class but also of a new social age group.

In Japan, beginning virtually any type of lessons involves the process of gaining membership in a new social group. The *minarai kikan,* or period of learning through watching, also involves long hours of standing on the sidelines and waiting to be accepted by the teacher and one's older peers. Although in formal settings, such as preschool and elementary school, this acceptance is eventually bestowed automatically, there is still a clearly defined period of watching as an unskilled outsider the graceful execution of school activities and routines by older peers before assuming a new social identity and gaining membership in the group. In this manner the cultural structuring of the process of group membership and activities serves to arouse and maintain individual motivation to participate in the learning process.

Inculcation of Basic Routines. The next step in the process of learning Suzuki piano or violin epitomizes the process of training the novice in basic routines that form both the components of the skill to be learned and a cognitive support system for the learning process. When the teacher determines that the child has developed sufficient concentration and motivation to join the lesson group, the child is called from the observers' seat and asked if he or she would like to take lessons along with his or her mother and the other children. With the proud mother looking on, the teacher introduces the child to the rest of the group, and the first lesson begins. The first lessons focus exclusively on training in basic routines and learning skills and have nothing to do with making sounds on the instrument. In the Suzuki method this begins with the process of teaching the child to bow in the style of traditional Japanese greeting. In a carefully choreographed ritual similar to a ballet routine, the child is taught to put the feet carefully together, place the hands on the thighs, straighten the body, and then incline the torso at the correct angle and hold for a count of three. On straightening, the child looks at the teacher and says clearly *"Onegai shimasu"*—which could be loosely translated as "Please teach me." One step at a time, the act of bowing is broken down and taught as a ritualized dance: "Feet, one, two. Hands on thighs. Bend, one, two, three. Straighten. *Onegai shimasu.*" The first lesson ends with the teacher asking the child to promise to practice carefully every day according to the mother's instructions until he or she can perform the bow smoothly at the next lesson.

This apparently simple task is in fact very complex. Besides posing a considerable challenge to the physical coordination of a two- to four-year old child, it forces the child to consciously monitor and adjust bodily movements according to a verbally cued model. This is initally practiced on a large-motor scale involving the torso, legs, and arms, before proceeding to control the wrists and fingertips on the instrument itself. This initial stage of lessons is considered extremely important in developing a proper attitude toward the learning task itself. Beginning each lesson with a properly respectful request for instruction requires the child to reaffirm his or her commitment to the learning process and is seen as important in establishing a serious mindset. Also, the child begins the establishment of a habit of careful, daily home practice or study immediately on induction into the lesson situation and learns to accept practice as a responsibility concomitant with the lesson process.

This stage of learning is almost exactly replicated in most early educational settings, particularly first-grade classes. During the first few days of school, the class practices countless times how to stand, bow, and recite "Good morning, teacher" in unison. The process of standing up, bowing, and sitting down again is similarly choreographed into a series of tiny precise steps in which every move is calculated—even whether one arises from the right or left side of the chair. Every routine basic to daily classroom life is broken down into a similar series of careful steps, painstakingly practiced again and again until it become second nature, and then speeded up again until it becomes an automatic, smoothly executed part of the school day.

First-grade students practice how to prepare their desk top and come to order before class starts. For several days before actual instruction begins, students practice together a routine in which they place their textbook on the left side of their desk, notebook in the center, and pencil and eraser horizontally at the top right of the desk. Each desk is identically arranged according to a diagram drawn on the board. Then the students sit with backs straight, hands on knees, and eyes on the teacher waiting for a signal to end the drill. After several consecutive days of repeated practice of this routine, students accomplish it automatically with the speed and assurance of a drill team, and the cueing is delegated to the daily student monitor.

Although the explicit training of such detailed routines seems uncomfortably rigid and authoritarian to the unaccustomed Western eye, in practice it actually reduces the amount of authority and control teachers must exercise on a daily basis. By carefully training students in the behavior expected of them and practicing it until it becomes an individually maintained habit, teachers avoid the necessity of using their own authority to bring the class to order and to personally direct the preparation of lesson materials. By expending extra time and effort in establishing learning routines at the beginning of a child's school career, for the rest of the child's public school life, within seconds after the teacher enters the classroom, the class calls itself to order and sits with all lesson materials prepared, ready for the teacher to begin.

Elementary school teachers share with Suzuki teachers the cultural belief in the importance of establishing the habit of conscientious daily home practice or study before introducing the main curriculum content. The guidelines distributed by local public elementary schools to parents of children entering first grade routinely describe the importance of training children in the habit of regular home study. In a typical memorandum from one school, parents are requested to begin training this habit six months before the first day of school by having their child write their name five times each day in their best handwriting in a blank notebook. This practice is to be continued each day without fail in the same notebook until the first day of school. This practice develops the habit of daily home study before the child reaches school, and it also allows the child to realize the importance of sustained diligent practice in improving performance by seeing the improvement in handwriting that occurs over the six-month period. Teachers assert that once students have thoroughly understood the effectiveness of diligent practice and developed the necessary daily habits, they become much more disciplined, self-motivated learners. For this reason, five to ten minutes of daily homework is commonly assigned in Japanese first grades.

Developing Concentration Skills. Once a new Suzuki student has learned to execute a proper bow, the next steps in the training process attempt to strengthen the child's ability to concentrate. This is done through carefully structuring the way in which the child mentally and physically prepares to play the instrument. Through a similar precisely choreographed ritual, the child learns to properly orient the body to the keyboard and hold the hand in the correct position above the key. Next, the mind is focused as well. The child is taught to focus the eyes on the back of the hand held over the key and to concentrate for a slow count of three. Then a one-and-a-half- to two-minute recording of the first song the child will learn is played, and the child holds the "ready" position with the eyes on the back of the hand until it is finished.

This task is challenging for a three-year-old and usually requires from two to six weeks, depending on the child. It requires learning to focus the child's mind on the task at hand and to ignore distracting thoughts and outside influences while on the piano bench. It is always approached in the manner of a personal and pleasurable challenge. The teacher gradually encourages the child to hold his or her concentration for slightly longer—a count of five instead of three, or for two phrases of the song instead of one. Each week generous praise greets slightly longer concentration ability, and the child is encouraged to compare this week's progress to that of the past week and to take personal pride in his or her increasing ability to accomplish a difficult task. Japanese teachers of all disciplines view the ability to concentrate as a skill that is developed by practice, rather than as a function of personality or the child's tendency to be obedient. Good concentration is always praised as *"jozu,"* or skillful, never with the observation, "You're being a good boy or girl." Children whose attention wanders easily are believed to be in need of concentration *practice* rather than *discipline.*

Similar concentration games and exercises were observed in preschool and first-grade classrooms. In the manner of a coach encouraging a group of beginning athletes, the teacher always structured the game in such a way that its daily repetition left a clear record of the class's growing skillfulness. Initial demands were always short but required complete immobility and quiet. Gradually the challenges lengthened until after several months, the entire class of first graders could stand at attention in school assemblies without moving or talking for as long as ten minutes.

Self Monitoring of Performance. In the Suzuki method, learning to play the first note comes almost as an anticlimax. After two to six months of careful preparation, the child is judged to have completed the prerequisites necessary to actually begin to make sounds on the piano or violin. However, the child's first production of sounds is structured in such a way as to establish a long-term habit of careful evaluation of his or her own performance. After the child properly orients body and hand to the instrument and rests the eyes on the hand, the teacher commands, "Listen," and plays the first note of the first song on the record, and there is a silence for a count of three. Then the child is instructed, "Ready"; then there is silence for a count of three; then "Play." The child plays the note and then there is an evaluative silence for a count of three; then again, "Listen"; the teacher plays; silence; "Ready"; silence; "Play"; silence. This sequence is repeated several times with the same note, and then the teacher stops and praises the good points of the child's performance and clearly tells the child what to change in the next attempt. Then the process begins again.

This procedure is maintained for every note that the child plays for the next several months and inculcates the habit of mindful concentration: first, to form a mental model of what will be produced, then to carefully prepare, then to execute, then to evaluate. Never is the child allowed to approach the instrument in a lackadaisical, half-attentive manner. In addition, the teacher clearly verbalizes the strong and weak points of the child's performance in such a manner that the child is encouraged by his or her growing ability but knows also what to work on.

To an American observer entering the lesson at this point, the tiny three- or four-year-old child perched on a high stool in front of a huge piano displays an almost unbelievable ability to concentrate. In the manner of a serious adult ten times the child's age, he or she responds quickly and accurately to the teacher's instructions, with eyes never leaving the keyboard. Both teacher and student are completely absorbed, and the lesson is surprisingly businesslike, with a minimum of the fun and games and sugar-coated sweetness Westerners usually associate with the training of preschool children. However, to the charge that the lessons do not seem "fun" in an American sense, Japanese Suzuki teachers point out that the children listen carefully, try hard, and practice willingly and well, and the enjoyment they derive is the personal satisfaction of competent execution and growing ability. Developing this attitude and the prerequisite learning abilities in children is the criterion for successful introduction to learning situations in Japanese teaching theory.

Preschools and first grades reflect this pervasive cultural emphasis on mindfulness in task preparation and evaluation. Initial speed in task performance is severely deemphasized in favor of extreme care and precision of execution. Throughout the school day, children are reminded again and again to take inventory of their materials and to be prepared for the new transition. Once the new task has begun, sloppy preparation is not cheerfully overlooked. In hundreds of hours of classroom observation, the only instances in which individual students were observed to be punished by being forced to stand or refrain from group participation were as a result of forgetting materials. Once a task has been executed, evaluation, or *hansei*, is a typical ritualized final step in the process. Group activities, ranging from daily cleaning of the classroom to the yearly class trip, end with a formal student-led period of *hansei*. Remedial pedagogy and discipline both focus on trying to get the student to reflect on and understand his or her inappropriate behavior and to develop an independent ability for self-evaluation.

Conclusion

Certain elements of these Japanese methods of training basic learning skills and attitudes bear some resemblance to individual aspects of various pedagogical techniques developed in the West. However, in the Japanese case, they represent a pervasive, universally recognized and almost unconscious cultural structuring of the basic goals and practices of early education. As a product of a long historical process of development, they form an integral part of the values by which Japanese adults unconsciously structure their own daily lives, as well as the ways they organize the process of cultural transmission to the young. Growing up in this environment, Japanese children receive both naturally acquired experience and consciously structured training in the development of proper attitudes and cognitive support skills for the learning process.

Recent Western interest in Japanese education has tended to focus on easily measurable aspects such as test scores, administrative organization, and curriculum content. However, closer observation reveals the existence of a fascinatingly different and yet highly sophisticated and effective indigenous educational ethno-psychology. The preliminary evidence presented in this chapter focuses on one aspect of this indigenous approach—training to facilitate the development of appropriate learning attitudes and cognitive support skills. It suggests that given appropriate training and environmental support, children may be able to develop sophisticated control of their learning behavior much earlier than is believed in the West. Perhaps this example will encourage Western educators and psychologists to reflect on the manner in which our own cultural assumptions about the teaching and learning process restrict our understanding of the limits of early experience and the development of children's abilities.

References

Comber, L. C., and Keeves, J. *Science Education in Nineteen Countries; An Empirical Study*. New York: Wiley, 1973.

Gardner, H. *Frames of Mind: The Theory of Multiple Intelligences*. New York: Basic Books, 1983.

Herrigel, E. *Zen in the Art of Archery*. London: Routledge & Kegan Paul, 1953.

Husen, T. (Ed.). *International Study of Achievement in Mathematics: A Comparison of Twelve Countries*. New York: Wiley, 1967.

Kojima, H. "A Cultural Background of Learning and Problem Solving in Japan." Paper presented at the Conference on Child Development in Japan, Ann Arbor, Michigan, April 1985.

LeVine, R. "Anthropology and Child Development." In C. M. Super and S. Harkness (Eds.), *Anthropological Perspectives on Child Development*. New Directions for Child Development, no. 8. San Francisco: Jossey-Bass, 1980.

Mead, M. *Growing Up in New Guinea*. New York: William Morrow, 1975.

Nagano, S. "Docility and Lack of Assertiveness: Possible Causes of Academic Success in Japanese Children." Paper presented at Stanford Conference on Child-rearing in Japan, March 1983.

Rohlen, T. *For Harmony and Strength*. Berkeley: University of California Press, 1974.

Salkind, N., Kojima, H., and Zelniker, T. "Cognitive Tempo in American, Japanese, and Israeli Children." *Child Development*, 1978, *49*, 1024–1027.

Stevenson, H. "Classroom Behavior and Achievement of Japanese, Chinese, and American Children." In R. Glazer (Ed.), *Advances in Instructional Psychology*. Hillsdale, N.J.: Erlbaum, 1985.

Stigler, J. W., Lee, S. Y., Lucker, G. W., and Stevenson, H. W. "Curriculum and Achievement in Mathematics: A Study of Elementary School Children in Japan, Taiwan, and the United States." *Journal of Educational Psychology*, 1983, *74*, 315–322.

Taniuchi, L. *Classroom Discipline and Management in Japanese Elementary Classrooms.* Washington, D.C.: United States Study of Education in Japan, National Institute of Education, 1985a.

Taniuchi, L. "Cultural Continuity in an Educational Institution: A Case Study of the Suzuki Method of Music Instruction." In M. I, White and S. Pollak (Eds.), *The Cultural Transition: Human Experience and Social Transformation in the Third World and Japan.* London: Routledge & Kegan Paul, 1985b.

Vogel, E. *Japan and Number One.* Cambridge, Mass.: Harvard University Press, 1979.

Lois Peak is program coordinator of the Middle Atlantic Region Japan in the Schools Program (Marjis). Her recently completed dissertation fieldwork focused on classroom management and behavioral control in Japanese preschools and first-grade classrooms. A recipient of grants from both the Japan Foundation and Harvard University, she received a doctoral degree in comparative human development from the Harvard Graduate School of Education in June 1986.

Index

128

Howe, M. J. A., 68, 84
Howes, C., 24, 30, 55, 64
Hubbard, E., 106
Hughes, M., 32, 46
Humphreys, L. G., 38, 46
Hunt, J. M., 1, 3, 6, 7, 8, 9, 31, 32, 33, 34, 35–36, 38, 39, 40, 41, 42, 46, 47, 49, 63, 88, 109
Husen, T., 113, 122
Hypatia, 94, 96, 99, 106, 107

I

Illinois, infant-care study in, 35, 37–39
Infant care: analysis of, 31–48; background on, 31–35; conclusion on, 44–46; cross-sectional study of, 35–37; educational, 37–39; findings on, 35–44; and social class and language skills, 39–40; studies of, 34–35; and tutored human enrichment, 41–44; and untutored human enrichment, 40–41
Intelligence: approaches to, 33–34; and distancing, 56–57, 60, 63; early development of, 68, 69; and early experiences, 88; and infant care, 33, 38, 39, 43, 45; and studies of early experience, 1–2, 3, 4
Iran, infant-care studies in, 35, 40–44
Israel, cognitive style in, 114–115
Itard, J., 106

J

Jacobi, C. G. J., 91, 93, 96, 99, 100, 102, 106, 107
Japan: distancing study in, 60; learning skills and attitudes in, 111–123
Japan Foundation, 111n
Jersild, A. T., 3, 9
Johnson, J. E., 56, 65
Juge-Chapsal, C., 106
Jung, C. G., 73

K

Kagan, B. F., 106
Kagan, J., 19, 29, 54, 64
Karnes, M. B., 33, 46
Kashiwagi, K., 60, 64

Kearsley, R. B., 19, 29
Keeling, S. V., 106
Keeves, J., 113, 122
Keister, M. E., 18, 29
Kelly, G. A., 50, 64
Kelly, J., 13, 30
Kelly, J. C., 83
Kennedy, J. F., 31
Kennedy family, 31, 74–75
Kirk, G. E., 39, 40, 46, 47
Klaus, R. A., 32, 46
Koenigsberger, L., 106
Kojima, H., 111n, 113, 114–115, 122
Kollros, L., 107
Kovalesky, S., 95, 96, 98, 99, 101, 102, 104, 105, 107
Krolick, G., 21, 30
Kusch, E., 107
Kuznetsov, B. G., 107

L

Labov, W., 39, 40, 47
Lagrange, J., 91, 92, 96, 99, 105, 106, 107, 109
Lamb, M., 20, 30
Laplace, P. S., 91, 93, 96, 99, 101, 102, 106
Launay, L. de, 107
Lazar, I., 25, 29, 88, 109
Learning skills and attitudes: analysis of training in, 111–123; background on, 111–113; and basic routines, 114, 117–119; and concentration, 119–120; conclusion on, 121–122; and motivation arousal, 114, 116–117; of novice students, 113–121; and self-monitoring, 114, 120–121
Lebanon, infant care in, 43
Lee, S. Y., 123
Leffler, A. C., 107
Leibniz, G. W., 91, 92, 96, 98, 99, 100, 101, 104, 106, 107, 108
Lenzer, I. I., 68, 84
Levenstein, P., 33, 47
LeVine, R. A., 83, 111n, 112, 122
Lewis, G., 107
Lieberman, C., 40, 46, 47
Lobatchevsky, N. I., 91, 93, 96, 99, 101, 105, 106, 107
Locke, J., 1